Paris Alliance israélite universelle

The Alliance Israélite Universelle

Publication of the twenty-fifth Anniversary of its Foundation

Paris Alliance israélite universelle

The Alliance Israélite Universelle
Publication of the twenty-fifth Anniversary of its Foundation

ISBN/EAN: 9783337061630

Printed in Europe, USA, Canada, Australia, Japan

Cover: Foto ©ninafisch / pixelio.de

More available books at **www.hansebooks.com**

THE

ALLIANCE ISRAÉLITE UNIVERSELLE

PUBLICATION

OF THE

Twenty-Fifth Anniversary of its Foundation

כל ישראל ערבים זה בזה

PARIS

AT THE SEAT OF THE SOCIETY

35, Rue de Trévise, 35

—

1885

ALLIANCE ISRAÉLITE UNIVERSELLE

FOUNDED IN 1860

~~~~~~~~~~~~~~~~~~~~~~~~~~~~~~~~~~~~~~

I

OBJECT AND ORGANISATION OF THE SOCIETY

Object of the work.

The *Alliance israélite universelle* was founded at Paris in 1860.

« To defend the honour of the Jewish name whenever attacked ; to encourage, by every possible means, labour and the exercise of useful trades and professions ; to fight, whenever necessary, against the ignorance and vice to which servitude gives rise ; to promote by the power of persuasion and moral influence the emancipation of our brethren who are still oppressed by the weight of exceptional legislation ; to push forward and consolidate perfect freedom by intellectual and moral regeneration : such is the work to which the *Alliance israélite universelle* has devoted itself. »

Thus expressed themselves the founders of the *Alliance* in 1860.

Their idea was condensed as follows in Article 1 of the Statutes :

The Association *Alliance israélite universelle* has for its object:

1° The promotion everywhere of the emancipation and moral progress of the Jewish people ;

2º To extend efficient aid to those who are suffering by reason of their being Jews ;

3º The encouragement of every publication calculated to promote this result.

This is a great and noble work, and there is no man, to whatever country, faith or philosophical doctrine he may belong, who cannot approve of, and join in it. The *Alliance* eagerly accepts the support of men of every faith and opinion. The success of the principles it is defending depends on the success which underlies all true morals. The Jewish cause is allied to the cause of civilisation. "We will have no other foe," said the founders of the Association, "than oppression ; no ally but persuasion ; no other standard than justice ; no other aim than the propagation of human fraternity."

Excluded Questions.

Political questions are entirely excluded, and find no place whatever in the programme of the Society.

The *Alliance* is and should remain aloof from the struggles of political and economic parties and nationalities, and must on account not become mixed up in them. It is elevated to a higher region, where all parties and political interests meet on the same footing of charity and humanity (1).

---

(1). Ad. Crémieux, Président of the *Alliance*, said at the general meeting of the Association on May 31, 1864 : " I call to our Association our brethren of every creed. Let them come to us ; let them give their support to this great work of civilisation and immense progress ! Let them come to us : with what eagerness would w· meet them ! When I had the happy thought to call to the aid of the Lebanon Christians the Israelites of the whole world, with what spontaneity rich and poor hastened with their gifts to respond to my voice ! Let us go forward in unison with every creed under one and the same banner : *Union and progress*, humanity's devise ". The *Alliance* contributed to the movement in favour of the Lebanon Christians by opening itself a special subscription.

2

It is a lay society and gives no special preference to religious work. It promulgates no religious propaganda outside of, nor supports any religious doctrine comprised by Judaism. Theology is a foreign to it as politics.

Titles and Devise.

Why is the *Alliance* JEWISH? why UNIVERSAL?

It is Jewish because the Israelites are persecuted, because they have to fight, even in civilised countries, against secular hatred and prejudices ; in other countries they are subjected to iniquitous laws ; and in others to most barbarous treatment. It is Jewish because, while receiving very good support from people stranger to the Jewish religion, it is among the Israelites it has found, not the most hearty, but the most numerous adhesions. It is to the Israelites of our lands that public opinion leaves the duty of protecting the oppressed Israelites : it would not pardon them if they failed in that duty (1).

All other beliefs in the world are represented by nations and Governments which support them. If the Christians suffer in the Mussulman world, all christendom is aroused. The French Government sends its armies to the aid of Christians in Syria ; every Protestant community can count upon the support of a Protestant Government ; Russia sustains the Grecian communities all over the world.

The simple existence of these Governments is a guarantee and protection to communities of the same rites. But the

1) " You are Jews ", said Ad. Crémieux at the general meeting of the *Alliance* on May 22, 1873, " and the question is to protect the Jews. If a persecution broke out against the Christians, I would say to you : rush to the aid of the Christians. This is what I said (in 1860) when odious persecution assailed the Christians of the East. Have we not all the same origin, Jews, Catholics, Protestants, sectaries of Mahomet ? Have we not all the same God for father ? Let us hold out a fraternal hand to our brothers of every creed. "

persecuted Jews can find no Power to protect them. It is to call to their aid public opinion, the Press, the sympathy of Governments that the *Alliance* has been constituted. It gratefully avows that it has never had to solicit in vain for support.

The *Alliance* is universal : that is to say, it is composed of representatives of every country. A work such as this could not, nor should not be confined to one country alone. It should be common to the philanthropists of every land. It is a patriotic duty that must be undertaken by all : it is one of the first duties of the citizen : such is the teaching of the *Alliance* in its scholastic establishments. Its pupils learn the language, history, and geography of Turkey in Turkey ; of Bulgaria and Roumelia in its Bulgarian and Roumelian schools ; of Morocco at Tangiers, Tetuan and Fez. It says to its members of various countries : Be French in France, Germans in Germany, Italians in Italy. The *Alliance* is itself a great school of civilisation. By developing every noble sentiment in the hearts of the Israelites, it cannot fail to strengthen in them that of patriotic duty.

The *Alliance* has adopted for its motto these words of an old Jewish doctor : " All Israelites are answerable for each other ". That responsibility was not sought by the Israelites, it is imposed upon them by necessity. " Do they not persist in seeing in them, " as the founders of the work remarked, " a race who voluntarily remain distinct, when in reality they only aspire to share with the peoples who have adopted them every thing that can be shared without violation of conscience ? Are we not isolated by laws and manners, whereas we are charged with seeking isolation as a condition of our religious existence ? " The grand idea of universal fraternity is the idea of the Jewish prophets !

Means of Action.

How is the *Alliance* accomplishing its work?

For furthering the emancipation of the Israelites the *Alliance* appeals to public opinion, which it limits itself to soliciting and enlightening, and also to the benevolence of the Governments.

The support of the liberal Press has never failed it. The generous action of European Governments is always manifested in favour of oppressed Jews in uncivilised countries. The *Alliance* has only to point out abuses and acts of violence to ensure a stop being put to them. Never has it had to address itself in vain, to the free nations of Europe in favour of persecuted Israelites! They have the support of France, England, Italy, Austria and Germany in every part of the world; of Spain in Morocco; of Belgium, Holland and Switzerland whenever they are appealed to ; of Turkey within the confines of its Empire and dependencies; they have had, on serious occasions, the support of Russia and Greece; the United States of America have frequently made their powerful voice heard in favour of religious liberty. How many evils have been stopped or averted by French, English, and Italian diplomatic agents, ambassadors, ministers and consuls on their own initiative, or on the demand of the Committees of the *Alliance* to their Governments! These are undeniable proofs of that spirit of equity and justice which honours our century.

For the moral and intellectual elevation of the Israelites the *Alliance* has created the school work. How this organisation is working, of what importance it is, what are its results will be noted later on in a special chapter of this report. It is necessary to closely study in order to appreciate the value of this whole of institutions the object of which is to convey to the Jewish people in Eastern and African, and soon also, if possible, in divers European countries, sound and healthy elementary instruction, a taste for manual industry and the means with which to carry it on. This work is crowned by the co-operation granted to Jewish science, and the encouragement given to scholars.

Thus is completed, not without great efforts, the programme of the *Alliance*.

Organisation.

The Society is directed by a Central Committee sitting in Paris. This Committee comprises members of every country, who are called to take part in its deliberations by correspondence, after inspection of the order of the day of each sitting, which is regularly communicated to them.

The Central Committee are in correspondence with the members through the medium of the regional and local committees. The grouping of these local committees around the regional committees are only operative through the initiative of the committees which, by their geographical situation, their authority, and, above all, by their activity, design for this work. It should be created by them, and not imposed.

The Central Committee is named by the universal vote of the members of the Society. The vote by regions or by countries, or the vote by assumption has been often proposed, notably in 1876 and in 1879, but the division by countries is contrary to the spirit of the *Alliance*, and presents, in its application, difficulties in establishing the proportionality in the representation. Thus, the assumption would deprive the members from exercising a precious control, which it would be dangerous to weaken.

The division into fractions of the Universal *Alliance*

into national Alliances was likewise proposed, in 1872, at Berlin, as well as in 1879; but it is in unity only that the *Alliance* finds its force and its moral strength. A division would only have for result to spread the forces, which, in their isolation, would remain sterile. The fundamental idea of the *Alliance* is unity : divide the *Alliance* would be to destroy it.

Progressive Development.

The first country, which, after France, rallied to the *Alliance*, and gave to it a large co-operation, is Italy. Thence came, with very important contributions, since the year 1864, Turkey, the Scandinavian States, and the Spanish communities of America, which has always shown towards the *Alliance* the most precious attachment ; then, from 1868, especially, Hungary, England, the Netherlands, Belgium, and Switzerland. The very adhesion of Germany dates from 1869, when the *Alliance* found in the much regretted Dr. Landsberg, rabbi of Liegnitz, an active and devoted coadjutor. The United States of America have given to the *Alliance*, from its origin, the warmest marks of their sympathy, and the Society has constantly received from the Israelites of these regions very useful subsidies.

We will here give, for the end of the year 1884, a table of the members, distributed by countries :

List of the members of the Alliance by countries.

Alsace-Lorraine.	1.365	Belgium	184
England and Colonies	50	Bosnia	17
Anhalt	23	Brazil.	44
Austria	157	Brunswick	35
Hungary	1.935	Bulgaria	883
Baden	602	Denmark	198
Bavaria.	2.522	Egypt	365

Spain and Colonies .	10	Peru	14
United States of		Portugal	15
America	696	Prussia	8.733
France and Colonies.	4.789	Roumania.	551
Greece	114	Roumelia	201
Hanover	154	Russia and Finland .	129
Hesse.	520	Saxony	121
Italy	709	Servia	40
Japan	1	Sweden	123
Luxembourg	51	Switzerland	497
Morocco	247	Tripoline	27
Mecklembourg . . .	38	Turkey in Asia . . .	383
Mexico	4	Turkey in Europe. .	1.936
New Grenada	19	Venezuela	26
Oldenbourg	20	Wurtemberg	404
Holland and Colonies	1.367		30.310

In the above table is not figured, or else for very insignificant ones, certain countries which in the other times were more largely represented, among them England and Austria.

Analogous Societies.

The English Israelites in 1871 created an institution bearing the title *Anglo-Jewish Association in connexion with the Israelite Universal Alliance*. This excellent society, which sprang from the *Israelite Alliance*, has the same object as the *Alliance*. It keeps up daily relations with the Central Committee, and furnishes every year to its several schools important subsidies, which gives to these institutions a grand development.

Two years later another society was formed at Vienna on the model of the *Alliance* under the name of *Israelitische Allianz zu Wien*. Its principal object is the amelioration of the condition of the Jews of the country, at the same time not forgetting the general interests of Judaism.

The Members. — The Budget.

Despite the separation of the English and Austrian Societies, the number of members belonging to the *Alliance* is continually increasing, as the following table will show (1):

YEARS	NUMBER OF MEMBERS	Subscriptions RECEIVED	RECEIPTS	EXPENSES
1862	1 112			
1863	1.386			
1864	2.878			
1865	3.900			
1866	4.610	28.452	35.410	23.283
1867	6 826	36.072	47.678	49.208
1868	9.158	46.367	67.028	60.411
1869	11 364	69.904	82.914	85.159
1870	12.526	79.352	99.363	90.937
1871	13.370	87.263	58.162	54.789
1872	14 797	78.068	95.978	83 710
1873	16.252	105.152	138.952	128.779
1874	18 226	113.384	154.744	149.715
1875	20.272	113.131	164.525	143.397
1876	20 312	121.813	155.626	144.350
1877	21.289	139.336	161.501	182.344
1878	19.297	145.215	183.950	159.691
1879	20 650	162.060	250.764	218 207
1880	22.443	165.997	280.013	251 510
1881	26.166	163.902	283.336	277.186
1882	27 225	182 497	293.309	333.209
1883	28.252	172 969	337.832	371.583
1884	28.416	228.727	408.727	433.728
1885	30.310			

It will be seen by the above table that the number of members has somewhat regularly increased. The stagna-

(1 In this table and all the following report the sums are always indicated by francs.

tion of 1876 and the diminution of 1878 and 1879 are purely apparent, and simply arise from the radiations which should have been made a long time ago. Since 1875 care has been taken to gradually efface those members who no longer figure on paper. Another cause of this same kind of error occurred in 1883, after the death of Dr. Landsberg, of Liegnitz, and was the cause of an apparent augmentation of nearly 4,000 members, in reality corresponding to a diminution of in the receipts.

The year 1871 was an exceptional year, and the figures will show the influence of the war on the Society at that epoch.

It will be remarked that, in 1879, the sum total of the receipts suddenly augmented by 50,000 francs (without counting 20,000 francs coming from the subscriptions), and that this augmentation was maintained and increased in the following years.

These augmentations are composed principally of the important annual subvention accorded by Baron de Hirsch since 1879, in furtherance of the work of apprenticeship in the East (at present more than 47,000 francs a year), of the constantly increasing subventions of the Anglo-Jewish Association for the schools ; in fine, since 1882, of subscriptions varying from 15,000 to 24,000 francs for the school at Jerusalem, of which the principal contribution is due to the Montagu Committee of London.

If the Central Committee has seen itself forced to maintain the equilibrium of its Budget, it has not, by a misunderstood economy, augmented its capital to the detriment of the institutions which it has created. It is undoubtedly to be wished that the *Alliance* possessed a capital which would assure its future, but this capital should come from grand and numerous donations ; it cannot be obtained by what is withdrawn from the annual receipts. The acquired capital was, on the 30th June, 1884, 259,578 francs. The capital would have been seriously affected by the deficit, in 1882 and 1883, but for the generosity of Baron de Hirsch, who came to the assistance of the Society in filling up the deficit of those years.

The Foundation of M. de Hirsch.

Baron de Hirsch did still more. In December, 1873, he gave a remittance of 1,000,000 fr. to the *Alliance* for the foundation which now bears his name, and which is solely destined for the development of schools in Turkey. Thanks to this Foundation, of which the annual revenue is more than 53,000 francs, added to the receipts and ex· penses of the preceding table, the *Alliance* has been able to create new schools in Turkey, enlarge those already existing, and, finally, brought its efforts to bear on the City of Constantinople, where the difficulties as regards schools are very great.

Annual Budget.

With this Foundation, the annual Budget of the *Alliance* can be actually established as nearly as follows :—

Receipts :

Annual subscriptions . . . . Fr.	190.000
Donations	:0.000
Divers revenues	44.000
Subventions to the Schools accruing from the Anglo-Jewish Association, the Montagu Committee, and from divers donations	40.000
M. de Hirsch for apprenticeship	47.000
Foundation Hirsch.	54.000
Perpetual subscriptions	5.000
	400.000

Expenses :

General expenses.	38.000
Printing of bulletins (monthly and quarterly) in French and German, expeditions, postage	16.000
Primary schools, apprenticeship, materials for the schools, voyages, and inspection	192.000
The School at Jerusalem.	34.500
Preparatory School for boys in Paris for the formation of professors	40.000
Preparatory School for Girls	14.000
Agricultural School at Jaffa.	40.000
Provident Bank for professors.	5.000
Ancient Russian work	8.000
Library	2.500
Subventions to learned and other publications.	5.000
Acquisitions of values for the perpetual subscriptions.	5.000
	400.000

It will thus be seen that on a Budget of 400,000 francs the annual subscriptions, including donations, figure for about the half of the receipts, the rest being represented, above all, by the concurrence of several societies, by the produce of the Foundation Hirsch, and by an important annual contribution of M. de Hirsch.

It will also be seen that the Budget of Expenses, likewise of 400,000 fr., may be resumed as follows : —

Administration and publications of the Society.	54.000
Values for perpetual subscriptions	5.000
Library and learned publications.	7.500
Schools and apprenticeship	333.500
	400.000

Thus, in an expenditure of 400,000 fr., 333,500 francs are destined solely for the work of education to which the *Alliance* has consecrated itself ; or, adding the

7,500 fr. for the libraries and learned publications,
341,000 fr. ; that is to say, about seven-eights are employed for works of instruction. The rest is absorbed by
the Administration, which is of a special character, on
whom the great publicity given to the Bulletins imposes
exceptional charges.

Divers Chapters of the Budget.

The Budget does not reserve any particular chapter for
publications but those of the *Alliance*, and for scientific
works. The *Alliance* does not possess any secret funds ;
the concurrence which has always been accorded to it by
the political Press is a concurrence absolutely disinterested.
It redounds to the honour of the Press in thus aiding the
triumph of civilisation and humanity.

The Budget has neither a chapter for benevolent purposes. The *Alliance* can, nevertheless, in exceptional circumstances, whenever a great calamity occurs in any of
the regions, come to the succour of the populations afflicted.
It is thus it successively opened subscriptions for the Israelites of different countries, — Turkey, Morocco, Persia,
Tunis, and Russia. At the same time the Society is fulfilling a work of general interest ; the questions of local or
individual interest being foreign to its programme.

The Coadjutors.

The chief auxiliaries of the Central Committee in the
work of propaganda, and in the effort to maintain and
enlarge the resources of the Society, are the district and
local committees. To their indefatigable efforts is due the
development and progress of all its institutions. It also
enjoys the co-operation of the Grand Rabbis and Rabbis
of every country, the administrators of Jewish communities
and societies, and all benevolent men devoted to Judaism.
It owes particular homage to those who are deceased : to

Dr. Landsberg, Rabbi at Liegnitz, the true apostle of the *Alliance* in Germany ; to Dr. Schwarz, Rabbi at Cologne; to the Rabbi Leopold Loew of Szegedin ; to Sir Francis Goldsmid of London, who has for so long lent it the assistance of his talent and influence; to Charles Netter, founder of the agricultural school of Jaffa ; to its illustrious presidents S. Munk, whose works have enriched science and glorified Judaism ; and to Adolphe Crémieux, who was for sixteen years the beloved, honoured and revered President of the *Alliance*.

Its thanks are also due to the societies which have so ably seconded it in its work : the *Anglo-Jewish Association* before all ; the *Consistoire Central des Israélites français ;* the *Board of Delegates* of New York, the remarkable activity of which is so well known, which instituted for the benefit of the Association the *Pourim* collect, and never ceases its work of propaganda; the American societies *B'nai B'rith* and *Kesher shel Barzel*, which have constantly given proofs of their interest to the Society ; to the *Board of Delegates,* of London, which for many years contributed to the maintenance of several schools in Morocco, and which even now grants a subsidy to an English school annexed to the school of the *Alliance* at Tangiers.

May they all receive the hearty testimony of the Committee and the expression of its gratitude !

II.

THE ISRAELITES IN THE EUROPEAN STATES

1. Roumania.

General situation.

The question of the Jews of Roumania and Servia has occupied the attention of the *Alliance* ever since its foundation. For seventeen years, and up to the Berlin Treaty, in 1878, the *Alliance* had incessantly exerted itself to the utmost to relieve the unfortunate Israelites of those countries, to protect them from persecution, and assist them in their efforts for freedom. This was the hardest and most painful task it has to fulfil.

Formation of Roumania.

Moldavia and Walachia, formerly separated and subjugated to Turkey, had just been constituted autonomous Principalities by the Treaty of Paris of 1856 and the Paris Convention of 1858. They were merely bound to Turkey by a purely nominal bond, and in 1859, by a clever political measure, united together in one Principality.

Illusions in regard to Roumania.

At this time Roumania was regarded in Europe as a country ripe for civilisation. For a number of years its statesmen, with a patriotic perseverance to which one cannot but render homage, had succeeded in winning the sympathy of public opinion. The French Press, especially, was smitten with this little people of Latin race and language, who appeared as a newly discovered brother-people. Nobody doubted but that Roumania, who seemed in particular to

2

take example by France, would show herself worthy of
the model, and apply to the Israelites the great principles
of emancipation which France had first proclaimed.

The emancipation of the Roumanian Jews seemed therefore assured, and was awaited with absolute confidence.
It was a matter of special importance for the Israelites.
Roumania seemed destined to enlarge the geographical
ground, then so narrow, on which the European Jews
were living under the protection of a Parliamentary Government and equitable laws, and to introduce into the
Eastern world, south and west, ideas of tolerance and religious liberty. This would have been a splendid *rôle* for
her, and all her friends will regret that she did not adopt it.

New Legislation

Disquieting symptoms, it is true, have been produced
since the constitution of Roumania. This country possesses, in Walachia as in Moldavia, an organic Regulation
elaborated in 1831, under sorrowful influences, and in
which are contained the most melancholy souvenirs of the
barbarous legislation to which the Israelites were subjected
in the middle ages. The majority of the laws of exception
created later on against the Roumanian Israelites are but
the reminiscences of this regulation, the plagiarisms due
to the canonic laws and to Russian legislation. As may
well be imagined, these ancient souvenirs were not to be
effaced in one day, and no one was greatly surprised that
Article 46 of the Paris Convention of August 19, 1858,
at the urgent request of the Roumanian delegates,
probably, while assuring to all Moldo-Walachians,
without distinction of creed, the enjoyment of civil rights,
only accorded the immediate enjoyment of political
rights to the Moldo-Walachians of christian rites, with the
added restriction that the enjoyment of these rights

could be extended to other religions by legislative provision. In the formulation of the Civil Code of 1864 (Article 6) this undecided provision was adopted, and measures (Art. 8, 9 and 16) added which apparently opened to Jews born in Roumania, although regarded as foreigners, an easy road to naturalisation. It appeared then that Roumania, after some delay designed to prepare the transitions, was preparing to emancipate the Israelites. What was known of the politicians and of Prince Jean Couza, who then governed the country, justified this hope.

M. Crémieux at Bucharest in 1866.

The members of the Central Committee of the *Alliance*, many of whom may formerly have seen the Roumanian statesmen in Paris, or, at any rate, had heard the echos of their conversations and excellent professions of faith, doubted least of all the good intentions of Roumania. When, in 1866, M. Ad. Crémieux, President of the *Alliance*, on his way to Constantinople, passed by way of Bucharest to plead the cause of the Israelites, he believed he was visiting a friendly country, and was not entirely wrong. He was received by the Ministers and Deputies, then sitting in Constituent Assembly, with most active marks of sympathy and demonstrations of affection, and was conducted into one of the rooms of the Assembly, where the Deputies pressed around him listening eagerly to his eloquent words ; it was at this time that the Constitution was being voted and the Ministry had introduced Article 6 according all civil and political rights to indigenous Jews M. Crémieux left Bucharest with the conviction that the Article 6 would be voted without difficulty.

Pillage of the Synagogue of Bucharest.

It was an illusion, and the awakening was cruel. Hardly had M. Crémieux left Bucharest when au *émeute* broke out against the Jews. On Saturday June 30, at the moment when the Constituent Assembly were deliberating on Article 6, the courtyard of the Chamber was invaded, a tumult was produced in the Chamber itself, the Ministry and the Deputies changed their attitude, Article 6 was withdrawn, and the rioters, intoxicated by their success, rushed to the Synagogue which had just been constructed by the Jews of Bucharest, and furiously demolished the building. This was the prologue to the drama which has since unrolled itself in Roumania.

New Policy.—Revolution of 1866

A new policy was now commenced in regard to the Jews. Under the despotic government of the Hospodars excesses were prevented, demagogic agitations were held in check, and the Prince, imbued with the sentiment of this responsibility, applied himself to maintaining order, calming the passions, and to settling, at least, by degrees, the Jewish question. The revolution which overturned Jean Couza (February 23, 1866), raised to power Prince Charles of Hohenzollern, to-day King of Roumania. The personal sentiments of King Charles are well-known ; he deeply deplores the violences from which the Jews of Roumania suffer and which so discredit his country ; but the enemies of the Jews preponderate in the country and the constitutional *régime* has placed the power in their hands.

Demagogic Intrigues.

They are the masters, thanks to an electoral system which delivers over the Jews as prey to the Third College, composed principally of merchants and manufacturers jealous of the commercial activity of the Israelites. Little by little the Jewish question is becoming the pivot of all the home policy of Roumania. It is invariably on this question that the Opposition attacks the Government in times of election ;

and the Government, more preoccupied with the triumphs of its partisans than with the future and good name of the country, triumphs over its adversaries by surrendering to them the Jews. The persecutions, the expulsions, the laws of exception, all emanated in times of election, and were for a long time but an instrument of warfare, the Jews being less the object than pretext. This adventurous policy has borne its fruits : by dint of playing with persecution they have unloosed it.

Legal Persecution.

It especially took an acute character in the years 1866-70. This was evinced at the same time in legislative measures and in acts of violence and disorder. The legal persecution, though less exciting the imagination, was a thousand times more murderous than the riots and expulsions, and is still continued in the present day. The Civil Code voted in 1864, the Communal Law of the same year, the old provisions of the rural law became, in spite of their text, instruments of persecution against the Jews. The Constitution of June 30, 1876, in its Article 7, since become famous, refused naturalisation to all foreigners who were not Christians, and all Jews were treated as foreigners. The administrative jurisprudence pretended, against all truth, that the ancient legislation was never abolished and that the Jews, as in the middle ages, had no right to live in the rural communes. It had at its disposition quite an arsenal of decrees, judgments and old circulars, which were exhumed for the occasion.

The Laws of Exception.

These documents being law, can be recapitulated in certain measures of violent iniquity. The Jews had no right of permanent domicile in the rural communes ; were not permitted to establish themselves in business, and, in the event of their settling in the said rural communes, administration could expulse them as vagabonds or on any other pretext ; they could not own houses, lands, vines nor real estate of any description, and were not permitted to possess houses and shops except in the towns ; they were not allowed to possess farm lands, could not keep hotels or wine-shops, nor be tenants of the grants or concessions of the rural communes. In fine, a law of April 13, 1873, outdoing the foregoing prohibitory measures, stated in its Article 8 : " In the rural communes, villages and hamlets, in inns or taverns isolated or situated on the high roads, no retailer of drinks can obtain a license unless he be inscribed on the communal electoral list of a Roumanian commune ". The right to deal in spirits was formerly the monopoly of the boyards, who usually rented to the Jews. By a stroke of the pen the law of 1873 reduced to destitution thousands of Jewish families.

The Jews of the towns are not less affected : they are refused the right to possess houses, or to take part in municipal elections. Needless to say that the Jews are excluded from all public functions and liberal careers : A Jew cannot be a solicitor, or apothecary, or railway servant, or dealer in tobacco, or take part in contracts for public works, or in those for land sold by the State. Before the tribunals or courts of law the Jew takes the oath *more judaïco* : if he has a christian servant he runs the risk, as happened in 1867 and 1872, of seeing resuscitated the old canonic provisions on the subject. The Jew has no rights, but he has to perform all the duties and bear all the burdens of the ordinary subject. He is amenable to military service the same as any other Roumanian ; but if he has the right to be killed for his country, he is debarred that of becoming a sub-lieutenant.

Again on March 15, 1884, a law on the pretended

peddling deprived 20,000 Roumanian Israelites of their means of subsistence. Never were they so cruelly hit; their misery was frightful, and ever since that epoch they have been writhing in intolerable sufferings!

Persecution by Riots.

This homicidal law, and all the economic laws that preceded it, has made, silently, more victims than all the riots and expulsions which formerly moved the public opinion. Of what use is it to recount here these painful and sorrowful episodes of the persecution? They are engraven on every memory. No one has forgotten the expulsions *en masse* of the spring of 1867, ordained by M. Jean Bratiano, and the drowning at Galatz, which was one of the most inhuman of acts; nor the events of 1868, the *émeute* of Berlad and Galatz, the Jassy expulsions, nor the cruel expulsions ordered in 1869 by M. Cogalniceano and renewed by the same Minister at the commencement of 1870; the bloody riots of the same year at Tecuch and Bacau, the disturbances more grave still in 1872, at Ismaïl, Cahoul and at Vilcov, *à propos* of a censor that a baptised Jew was accused of stealing from the Ismaïl Cathedral; nor, finally, in 1876 and at the commencement of 1877, the expulsions effected, during the electoral period, in the district of Vaslui, the disturbances at Jassy, and the *émeute* excited at Darabany by a noble lady, Mme. Smaranda Cimarra. These sad events have raised throughout the whole world a movement of reprobation and horror.

Action of the Alliance.

What, in the midst of these persecutions, was the conduct and the action of the *Alliance?* It commenced to occupy itself with the Roumanian Israelites with the favour of the Governments; it believed in the professions of faith of the statesmen of the country. When, in 1866, M. Crémieux, at Bucharest, took leave of the Deputies, he cried : " God bless Roumania ! " The *Alliance*, in Roumania, was ever but the adversary of the persecutions .

The European Powers.

Roumania existed, at that epoch, under the guarantee of the Powers, and they were conscious of their responsibility for the excesses she committed.

" This oppression cannot be tolerated, " said the Emperor Napoleon III to M. Crémieux, in 1867, and the *Exposé* of the situation of the French Empire of the same year speaks spontaneously " of the regrettable acts of religious intolerance which are being perpetrated in Roumania. " The European Powers could not bear the idea that such great atrocities could be committed, so to speak, under their patronage. It was indignation and sorrow which, on the expulsion of 1867, prompted the Identical Note of the European Consuls at Jassy on July 15, 1867, wherin these functionaries declared that it was " their rigorous duty to protest loudly against these acts of barbarity; " it was these sentiments which inspired the same functionaries in their Identical Note of April 15, 1868, on the events at Bacau ; the letter of M. de Moustier, Minister of Foreign Affairs for France, and the Note of Baron d'Eder, Agent and Consul-General for Austria, of April 24, 1868, relative to the same events ; and lastly, the Collective Note of the Consuls-General at Bucharest, of April 18, 1872, on the Ismaïl and Vilcov affairs and on the impunity accorded to the culprits.

A wise and moderate Government, instead of searching in these steps a subject for recrimination against the Powers or against foreigners, should have found, as it was the sole wish of those who made them, a basis of support and strength to calm the passions of the populace and settle with equity the Jewish question.

Artifices of the Persecution.

It was necessary, however, that the truth should be shown, and the function of the *Alliance* was to bring it to light. Nothing could equal the persistence of the Roumanian agents to misrepresent it. Thus the expulsions of 1867 were simple hygienic measures; the expulsions of 1868, of 1876-77, pure inventions, manœuvres to discredit Roumania. The persecuting laws were especially drawn up, and are still, with a view to mislead and impose upon opinion. The name of the Jews is not mentioned, but intolerance is hidden in the most delicate euphemisms. Naturalisation was refused not only to foreign Jews, but to all *foreigners who are not of christian rites;* residence in the country is accorded only to *persons inscribed on the communal electoral list;* the most ordinary artifice consists in disguising the Jews under the name of *foreigners.* For the Roumanians all Jews, even those who have been born from father to son in the country, and whose family has been established there from time immemoriable, are foreigners. It is a secret to nobody that all laws made in recent years against foreigners in general bear a false stamp: by foreigners they must only be understood to mean Roumanian Jews. The proceeding appeared in the first place clever, it is to day worn out. The disastrous law on peddling of 1883 has had no recourse to that artifice, it is a general law made for all inhabitants of the country, foreign and native alike. The thing is to know how to apply it. It contains sufficient exceptions to put the Administration at ease; it strikes only those whom it is intended to strike.

Public Opinion and the Chambers.

In enlightening the Press, the Governments, and public opinion on the real state of things in Roumania, the sense and bearing of their legislation against the pretended foreigners, the violence of the *émeutes* and acts of persecution, the *Alliance* thinks it has contributed to sometimes prevent some of these great evils, and to attenuate those which it was unable to prevent. Minister Bratiano retired after the scandal of the expulsions of 1867, and Minister Cogalniceano after those of 1869-70. The interpellations made in the House of Lords, at London, on July, 1, 1867, by Lord Stratford de Redcliffe ; in the House of Commons, by Sir Francis Goldsmid, member of the Central Committee and later of the Anglo-Jewish Association, on April 24, 1868, and April 19, 1872 ; that of Godefroi in the Chamber of the Netherlands, September 23, 1872, disperse all obscurities accumulated around this question. No one any longer doubts the reality of these persecutions for so long and so obstinately denied. The Jewish cause was won in face of public opinion. They had already previously received a precious testimony by the nomination of an Israelite, Mr. B. Peixotto, to the post of Consul-General of the United States of America to Bucharest.

Meeting at Paris in 1876.

The events which took place in Turkey in 1876, the Turkish war against Servia and Montenegro, followed by the Constantinople Conference, seemed to afford the Western Israelites an opportunity to act in favour of their Roumanian coreligionists. ·

On the proposition of the *Anglo-Jewish Association*, the *Alliance* convened at Paris on December 11, 1876, a meeting composed of delegates of various European States and of America, which was engaged for several days in deliberating on this serious question. The meeting drew up a Memorandum, wich was presented by the late Charles Netter to the several members of the Conference at Constantinople.

The Berlin Congress.

Everybody is aware of the failure of the Conference at Constantinople, which resulted in the Russo-Turkish war. When the Berlin Conference assembled in 1878 to settle the Eastern Question, the Central Committee addressed a Memorandum to the Congress to which all the members who had taken part in the meeting of 1876 had given their adhesion. The Central Committee furthermore deputed Mr. Kann, the late Charles Netter and Mr. E. F. Veneziani to proceed to Berlin to uphold, before the members of the Congress, interests of Eastern Jews generally and particularly of those of Roumanian nationality.

Their cause was won in advance. On the initiative of the French Government, the Congress, in proclaiming the independence of Servia and Roumania, and organizing Bulgaria and Eastern Roumelia, declared that in those States " the distinction of religious beliefs and professions of faith could not be urged as a motive for exclusion or disability as far as the enjoyment of civil and political rights was concerned". These provisions constitute Articles 5, 20, 35 and 44 of the Berlin Treaty, signed on July 13, 1878. This was a great victory, and the reward of fifteen years of continuous struggles and exertion. United Europe established in the East the equality before the law of all religious beliefs and proclaimed the emancipation of the Jews. This great act is unique in the history of Judaism, and constitutes a most solemn charter of its enfranchisement.

Results of the Congress.

A fresh meeting was convoked by the *Alliance* at Paris, in 1878. No one entertained any illusion as to the difficulties the application of the Treaty would encounter in Roumania. At this very time she was negotiating with several Powers with the view of concluding treaties of commerce, while intending to apply her intolerant legislation even to the Jews of other countries. Several States—notably Austria-Hungary and Russia—signed this treaty. Others, however, preferred to wait till the Roumanians should begin to execute the Berlin Treaty.

Suppression of Article 7 of the Constitution.

The Treaty of Berlin stipulated for the annulment of all exceptional laws against the Roumanian Israelites. The Government never had the least intention of conforming to this stipulation. Instead of proclaiming Roumanian citizens all Jews born from father to son in the country, it continued to treat them as foreigners, and only cancelled Article 7, prohibiting the naturalisation of foreign Israelites. The Powers were not deceived, and refused to accredit Ministers to Roumania.

The Roumanian Chamber decided to make a semblance of concession, and Art. 7 was abrogated, after the discussions which had agitated the country during a whole year, in October, 1879. A special article in the new law accorded naturalisation in a lump to 883 Jewish soldiers who had served in the last war, and about fifty Roumanian Israelites have since been naturalised by the Chambers, and this is how Roumania executed the Treaty of Berlin! The 883 Jewish soldiers were not able to obtain their naturalisation, the municipalities having refused them the necessary documents for the purpose of establishing their identity.

The Actual Situation.

Nevertheless, a great progress was made, and had it not been for the fatal law on hawking, which came to awaken anew our fears and our sufferings, the Roumanian question might have been considered as having entered on a new phase. With the abolition of Art. 7, with the Treaty of Berlin, and Art. 8 of the civil code which gave to every person born and brought up in Roumania the right of reclaiming, on his attaining his majority, his rights as a native, the Roumanian Israelites held in their hands the instrument which would have prepared them for complete emancipation. There is no legal obstacle to prevent them from recognising the rights which belong to them. And yet they still suffer cruelly. Legal persecutions still go on, and they are reduced to famine; already, the mortality is very great among them; in a few years, and they will be decimated by misery. It is a harrowing spectacle to see this active, laborious, and intelligent population reduced to mendicity by a law without pity. The Jews have on their side justice, right, the Constitution, treaties, and the public opinion of the world.

2. SERVIA.

The Situation.

The question of the Jews in Servia has never partaken of the same amount of gravity as in Roumania. The reason is, perhaps, to be found in the character of the Servian people, in its political organisation, and in the firmness of its Government; in fine, in the small number of Servians Jews, at the most 1,500 or 1,800 souls. The sufferings and the humiliations they have endured have, however, not been wanting.

The Cause of the Persecutions.

In Servia, as in Roumania, the source of these persecutions is to be found in the paltry meanness and jealousy of its merchants and tradesmen.

" What is, said in 1863 Mr. Ricketts, English Consular " Agent at Belgrade, the motive of these persecutions " against the Jews?

" I have put this question to several persons, and they " have all come to the conclusion that the Jews in this " country, as in a great number of others, are a peaceful " and industrious people. They lend money, it is true, " but always at the ordinary rate of the country. It " is also the Jews who furnish to the peasants of the inte- " rior the merchandise of which they stand in need. The " prosperity which the Jewish inhabitants owe to this kind " of commerce is looked upon with a jealous eye by Servian " merchants ; and a great many of these last mentioned, " who do not in any way shine by a spirit of charity, " would be glad to see these poor Jews chased from the " country. "

It is no longer the same at the present day. Experience has shown, in Servia at least, the puerility and the inconvenience of these economical theories.

Historical. — Legislation.

In 1860, these theories were still in full favour, and the Jews were obliged to submit to their sad effects.

Under the dynasty of the Obrenowitz, and up to the epoch when it was overthrown by that of Kara-George, the sufferings of the Jews were insupportable. The *oustav* of 1838, made by the Sultan in favour of Servia, had accorded the same rights to all the inhabitants of the country ; Art. 28 of the Treaty of Paris of 1856, which was as important for Servia as for Roumania, had proclaimed unrestricted liberty for all kind of religions. Everything seemed to be regulated for the purpose of assuring to the Jews the full enjoyment of their civil and political rights.

Laws of 1856 and 1861.

These concessions were not of long duration. In the very year which saw the signing of the above Treaty of Paris, the 30th of October, 1856, a law, renewed in 1861, interdicted to all Jews a free residence in the interior of the country, only allowing them to live in the different towns where they were established, and refusing access to the country for all other Jews. The Constitution of the 11th of July, 1869, Art. 132, preserved these dispositions, and if they are no longer applicable at the present day, they are still duly inscribed in the law.

This law struck the Jews in their civil rights; their political rights have never been contested, at least in prac- tice. They always took part, as electors and eligible, in the municipal elections as also in the legislative ones. One Abraham Osor, a Jew, was elected a member of the Great Skuptchina assembled on the 28th February, 1877 ; and this same Jew and another named Moustapha, of Nish, were designated by the Prince as members of the Skuptchina which met on the 30th of December, 1880. The Jews form part of the army, and a great number of them served, during the war of 1876 and 1877, in the artillery, the baggage train, cavalry and infantry; four amongst them have been decorated, two as military sur- geons, and two others for feats of arms, and nothing shows that the Jews may not attain, at least at the pre- sent day, positions in the upper grades of the army.

Persecutions.

The most painful period in the history of the Jews of Servia was that which dates from the acces-ion to the throne

of Alexandre Kara-George in 1842, up to the lats war. At
the commencement of the century, under the Obrenowitz
dynasty, they were treated with kindness, and enjoyed the
same rights as their fellow-citizens. After the revolution
of 1842, the Prince, who was at the discretion of the different merchants, saw himself obliged to persecute them :
they were chased from all the towns in the interior, and
the entire body of them relegated to one of the most
miserable quarters of Belgrade. In 1856, even at the moment when the Treaty of Paris seemed to open to the Jews
of Servia an era of liberty, Kara-George consecrated by a
law the offensive practices of the Administration towards
them, followed by their expulsion from the towns in the interior. When, in January, 1859, the aged Milosch
remounted the throne, he sought to repair the evil, but his
son, Prince Michel, had not the moral force to thwart the
reclamations put forth by the Servian merchants. A few
months after his accession, the Jews were expelled from all
the towns in the interior (April, 1861). Other expulsions
followed in 1862, 1863, 1873, 1874, and again in 1877.
The Constitution of 1869 not having made any change in
the position of the Servian Jews, their situation remained
in the same up to the Treaty of Berlin.

Action of the Alliance.

The Princes of Servia have always welcomed in a friendly
spirit the steps taken in favour of the Israelites and the
counsels of the guaranteeing Powers as regard the Treaty
of Paris. The grievances manifested by the *Alliance* in
the years 1863 and 1864; the petition addressed by that
body in 1864 to the Servian Assembly ; the interpellation
made by Sir Francis Goldsmid to the English Parliament
on the 29th of March, 1867, followed by the steps taken by
a member of the Central Committee, M. de Camondo, at

Constantinople, before the Prince Michel, have contributed to enlighten the Servian Government on the situation of the Jews, and on the necessity of adopting a system of political liberty and tolerance. The protest of the four Great Powers, England, Austria, France, and Italy, on the 22d of September, 1869, against the maintenance of the illiberal laws in the Constitution of 1856 and 1861, has shown, in this question, the opinion of Europe. Prince Milan, who actually reigns, has always declared that the emancipation of the Servian Jews would be accomplished at no distant period, and he warmly approved the steps taken near his own person, at Paris in the autumn of 1873, and at Constantinople in 1874. Again, in 1880, he gave to a member of the Central Committee, Mr. S. E. Kann, the very best assurances as regarded the future of the Servian Israelites.

The Treaty of Berlin and its Effects.

Since the Treaty of Berlin, their emancipation has been accomplished, and has passed into the region of facts ; Article 35 of the Treaty, which stipulates a complete equality in favour of all Servian Israelites, is loyaly executed. Thus the laws of 1856 and 1861 may be considered as virtually abolished, although they are already inscribed in the Constitution, their abrogation clearly resulting from the acceptance of the Treaty of Berlin. The question of Servian Israelites can therefore be regarded as settled with honour for King Milan, his government and Servian people.

3. EASTERN ROUMELIA AND BULGARIA

These two principalities have been constituted by the Treaty of Berlin, with the same stipulations as for Servia and Roumania. The Constitution given to itself by Bul-

garia in March, 1879, recognised, by its Article 53, that
all persons born in Bulgaria not being under foreign
protection are Bulgarian subjects, and, by Article 57,
that all Bulgarians are equal before the law. The Constitution of Eastern Roumelia, elaborated in January, 1879,
contained the same dispositions under another form: `` I
shall love all my subjects without religious distinction,
said His Highness the Prince of Bulgaria to the Chief
Rabbi of Sofia, the laws shall be the same for all.'' It
was not without emotion that the Jewish Bulgarian families
saw depart for the first time, in 1879, the Israelitish
conscripts, but all understood what they owed to their
native country, and that fellowship in civil life is prepared
and sealed fellowship under the flag. The Bulgarian
Israelites are electors, they interest themselves in the
public affairs of their country ; three Israelites have taken
part, since 1880, in the Municipal Council of Sofia; the
Government accords a subvention to the Chief Rabbi, the
inspectors visit the schools of the *Alliance* and interest
themselves therein ; a difficulty which cropped up in 1880
on the question of market day, that certain municipalities
had fixed Saturday to mislead the Israelites, seems to
have been partly averted by the benevolent intervention
of the Prince; and also the absurd accusation of the use
of Christian blood, attempted at Sofia, in April, 1884, by
several malevolent individuals, has been promptly
arrested owing to the energetic measures of the authorities
and to the excellent attitude of the clergy and the press.
At the moment of the publication of this report the Bulgarian communities are reunited, with Government assent,
to furnish a central administration, a regular organisation,
put at their head a Chief Rabbi who will direct them in
the way of progress and help them to dissipate, by his
action towards the authorities, the prejudices which some-

times appear among the people and in the press. The Israelites of Bulgaria and Roumelia accomplish their patriotic duties, assimilate the national manners, and their relations with their fellow-citizens are excellent. The two countries practise, with the best sentiments of fellowship, the theories of equality of all those inscribed in their laws and march loyally in the way of civilisation.

4. Russia.

Old Relations with the Alliance.

It was a time when the action of the *Alliance* was regarded with favour by the Russian Government, an epoch contemporary with the foundation of the Society. In the affair of the Jews of Saratoff, unjustly condemned under the accusation of having killed a Christian infant, the Ambassador of His Imperial Majesty in Paris willingly offered the Committee excellent insurances. The memoir sent by the Committee on that occasion to the Emperor, in 1862, was the object of the attention of the Government, and later, in June, 1868, on a petition of M. Ad. Crémieux, the last survivor of the poor condemned ones, who had been transported to Siberia, was pardoned by the Emperor. In 1866, also, M. de Budberg, Russian Ambassador in Paris, transmitted a petition in favour of an Israelite of Minsk condemned to death, which was followed by a commutation of sentence. The same Baron de Budberg consented, on the demand of the Committee, to open an inquiry, in 1868, on the case of a young Israelite girl baptised against the wish of her parents. The Central Committee recalls these memories with a sentiment of lively gratitude.

What good might it not do if it could exercise its action towards the Russian Israelites, if its help could reach them, if it could help in the organisation of schools, professional works, agricultural institutions, work with them to their raising up again! Not being able to penetrate into Russia, where its publications even are interdicted, it is obliged to stop at the frontier and to content itself with exercising outside an action which, weak though it is, has not been without utility.

Famine of 1869.

Two great calamities have afflicted the Russian Israelites at two different times : famine in 1869, and the atrocious persecutions of the years 1881-82.

The famine of 1869 had revealed the frightful misery of the Israelites of Poland, heaped the one on the other in that region of the west from which they are forbidden to depart for other provinces. The sufferings from want had found numerous victims, the number of abandoned orphans was great, and the *Alliance* made. an appeal in favour of the Russian Israelites which was heard, a large subscription permitting it to aleviate the sufferings of famine and to seek an efficacious remedy for a chronic state of misery.

Meeting at Berlin.

A meeting composed of a delegation of the *Alliance* headed by its president, Adolphe Crémieux, of members of the Committees of the *Alliance* of Berlin, Kœnigsberg, and other towns, took place at Berlin in October, 1869. Two members of the Committee, Messrs. N. Leven and Léonce Lehmann, visited the towns the most tried by the plague and joined the elements of an inquiry on the situation of the Jews and the means of remedying it. Divers projects were proposed, the greater part excellent, if they had not encountered an obstacle in the legislation of the country. They wished to encourage agriculture, but Jews are forbidden to acquire rural property; to teach

them trades, but there is a want of work in those impo-
verished regions; to emigrate them to the interior, but the
law formally opposes it; to encourage emigration outside,
but such emigration is difficult and onerous. The meeting
at Berlin confined itself to the following measures :

1º To send to America, a country where the law protects
the liberty of each man and assures him the fruits of his
labour, a small number of Russian families who should
establish themselves there with the concurrence of American Israelites, and who, if they succeeded with the
resources furnished by the *Alliance*, would become little
by little a centre of attraction for their coreligionists.
They would also create a continuous current of emigration from Russia to the United States.

2º To establish at Kœnigsberg and in other towns a
work of apprenticeship where Russian-Polish children
should be particularly brought up.

The Kœnigsberg Committee.

The measures were put into execution. A special
Committee, established at Kœnigsberg, under the name of
the Principal Committee, was charged to execute them.

In less than a year, 675 emigrants were established in
America, where the Board of Delegates received them and
afforded them aid. Two hundred and twenty orphans were
placed by the Central Committee in different communities or
adopted by private individuals. A Committee of apprenticeship was established at Kœnigsberg, another at Memel,
and a third at Cologne. In 1873, the number of persons
sent to America was 800 ; the number of children placed in
different communities, 300.

Work of the Russian Apprentices.

The work of the Russian apprentices, nevertheless, continued to subsist; it is kept up by the ordinary resources

of the *Alliance*, which are inscribed in their Budget. The Principal Committee at Kœnigsberg has always under its direction from 55 to 60 children, who frequent the primary school and are taught different trades. Dr. Rülf, of Memel, on his part, since 1869, has opened a primary school for Russian children, which is subventioned by the *Alliance*. The Cologne Committee continue to afford aid towards the apprenticeship and education of Russian children; in fine, within the last few years a subvention has been accorded, for the same object, to Dr. Feilchenfeld, President of the *Alliance* at Posen. The results of the work have never for one moment been in doubt; the education given to these children naturally reaching on their families in Russia, in whose centre they will return. It is a useful work.

The Great Persecution of 1881-1882.

Much more serious has it been, in its origin as well as in its effects, the great catastrophe of 1881-1882. All the horrors of a barbarian epoch that were supposed to have disappeared for ever have been renewed; from Ekateri-noslaw to Vilna, bands of rioters have fallen upon the Jews. Who does not remember these bloody scenes of murder, pillage, incendiarism, and destruction! There has never been seen, in our century, a similar explosion of fanaticism and brutality.

A cry of indignation was raised throughout the whole of world! The unheard of cruelties committed without any reason or pretext, insufficiently repressed, and in many cases encouraged by subaltern agents in power, even excused by Ministerial acts, tended to raise an universal cry of reprobation. This cry found its highest expression in the admirable meeting held at the Mansion House in London, in February, 1882. Every friend of civilisation was touched to see drawn together all the great political men of

England, and the highest dignitaries among the clergy, to
solemnly protest in the name of justice and of humanity.

Subscriptions and Special Committees.

It was not sufficient simply to compassionate these victims of persecution, it was necessary to afford them relief.
Special Committees, in which all religions were represented, were organised for this object in England, France,
Germany, Austria, Italy, Belgium, Holland, Switzerland,
Denmark, and America. The London Committee was
presided over by the Lord Mayor; a Committee sitting at
Paris had at its head Victor Hugo. The two subscriptions
opened by the *Alliance* permitted it to place at the disposition of the work of succour a sum of more than one
million and a half of francs; and a further million was
placed at the disposal of the Society by Baron de Hirsch.
With these resources the Society was enabled to repair in
part the immense disaster, and bring about a relief.

What was to be done?

A considerable number of the unfortunates, flying
from these persecutions, were crowded into the towns on
the frontier; it was necessary to support them. It was
impossible of sending them to their homes, which no longer
existed; all the means of existence had disappeared for
them. As there was no more resources for the Israelites
in their own country, emigration was thought of.

Emigration to Palestine Impossible.

To what point must they be directed? Towards Palestine? No; Palestine is a poor country, where there are no
industrial establishments, no commerce, no roads, nor
other means of communication. The emigrants would
only augment the misery already so great among the
Israelites of the country. Less than anywhere, perhaps, was

it possible to found there agricultural colonies; a good soil
is rare; water, the materials necessary for construction
equally so ; implements of industry is to be sought
elsewhere; even the Arabs, despite their vigour, despite
their knowledge of the climate and the cultivation appropriate to the country, they only vegetated.

Emigration to America.

Emigration to America was only to be thought of seriously, a rich and immense country, where all labouring
men find, with their subsistence, the blessings of a régime
of liberty, where the victims of religious persecution are
sure to encounter public sympathy and the support of
their coreligionists. It was, then, towards the United
States of America that the *Alliance*, encouraged by the
experience of 1869, decided to send the Russian Israelite
emigrants. The Board of Delegates of New York promised
to receive these able-bodied men, capable of working.
This Board, the Hebrew Emigrant Aid Society (up to the
time when it was dissolved), the Hebrew Charities Society,
the excellent Committee of Philadelphia, and again other
Committees put forward their efforts in favour of the
emigrants.

Charles Netter at Brody.

It only remained to organise the emigration. Mr. Charles
Netter proceeded to Brody; he himself chose the emigrants,
and, at the end of a few months, with the aid of the Committees of Brody, Liegnitz, Breslau, Berlin, Antwerp, and
Hamburg, with the aid given by the American Committees,
two thousand persons were sent by the *Alliance* to America.
The choice made of these emigrants was so serious and ju-
dicious that nearly all of them succeeded, and only a few
returned to Europe. The work accomplished by M. Netter

was prodigious, but it was fatal to his health ; a few months later, and M. Netter was lost to the *Alliance!*

New Difficulties.

It was possible to believe that the work at Brody had terminated when the persecutions in the spring of 1882 threw into Gallicia an extraordinary mass of Russian Israelites assembled at Brody and at Lemberg ; their number, increasing little by little, was raised to 20,000 persons. The situation became serious ; it was necessary to take the necessary measures. A meeting was convoked at Berlin on the 23d of April, and it was resolved to continue the emigration, the special Committees of London, Paris, Vienna, and other towns offering their pecuniary services. The Mansion House Committee alone sent to the United States of America, to Canada, and other countries, up to July, 1882, more than 8,000 refugees.

Mr. Veneziani at Brody.

There were still 12,000 refugees at Brody. It was then that M. Veneziani, member of the Central Committee, visited that town in the name of the *Alliance* and of Baron de Hirsch. A change had taken place in the dispositions of the Russian Government, Count Ignatieff had given in his demission, and had been replaced by Count Tolstoï. The riots had ceased, and the return of the refugees to their native land had become possible. M. Veneziani caused the return to Russia of those persons who were incapable of emigrating to any good purpose. He caused the emigration to America of a certain number of other refugees ; the Special Committee of Paris brought 500 more which he took under his charge, in concert with the *Alliance*, besides the 1,000 which he had already collected, and, lastly, the *Alliance* placed a certain number in the Israelitish communities of France. In the month of October M. Veneziani had the

---

happiness of announcing to the Central Committee that there was not a single refugee left at Brody.

Agricultural Colonies in America.

With the sums collected in America itself and those which had been sent there by the *Alliance* and other European Committees, the emigrants have been helped and placed in agricultural and industrial establishments in America. Small agricultural colonies were organised in a certain number of localities : the *Alliance* colony at Vineland ; the Crémieux colony ; Bethlehem-Juda, near Mitchell and Mount Vernon, on the Dakota territory ; the New Odessa Colony, near Zeland, in the Oregon ; the Montefiore and Lasker colonies in Kansas, not far from that of Dakota ; other less important colonies, one 145 kilometres from Washington ; the Water View colony, near Baltimore ; the colony of Cotopaxi, in Colorado ; and a little colony in Independence country, in Arkansas.

Also the *Alliance* has several times seconded a very iteresting agricultural colony installed by Dr. Wechsler, Rabbi at St. Paul, at Painted Woods, Minnesota. The whole of these colonies forms a population of about 200 families or 1,000 persons. The other refugees have been placed in industrial or commercial concerns.

Agricultural Colonies in Palestine.

A number of Russian refugees bent their steps towards Palestine. Among others they founded there, near Jaffa, a colony called *Rischon-le-Zion ;* it is in the way of organisation. The Roumanian Israelites, driven from their country by misery, have created two colonies, one of which, *Rosch Pinnah,* is in the neighbourhood of Safed, and the other, *Samarin,* is at several kilometres from Caïffa. They form together a group of 92 families. These colonies are the work of a Roumanian Committee enticed by the idea of an agricultural establishment in Palestine, but the insufficient resources of these emigrants would have proved fatal to them if help had not reached them from elsewhere. Thanks to this succour, their success has become possible, but should not be an encouragement to emigration to Palestine, where it encounters obstacles without number.

What of the Future?

What, however, will the situation of the Jews in Russia become? It is very unhappy! A commission was named two years ago to study the legislation which governs them. The commission numbers among its members some eminent names. One of them, Prince Demidoff San Donato, published, in 1884, an excellent study on the Jews, in which he claims for them emancipation, liberty of living in all Russia, and common right.

These ideas are indulged in by other members of the commission. May they bear fruit ! The emancipation of the Russian Jews would put an end to a dolorous question from which Russia has suffered so long, and would be of the greatest benefit to the entire country.

III

MUSSULMAN COUNTRIES

1. TURKEY

The Government.

When, after having passed in review the situation of the
Israelites in certain countries, we pass on to Turkey, we
experience a sentiment of relief. There are no exclusive
laws against the Jews, there no legal persecutions, no vex-
ations on the part of the Government nor prejudices on
the part of the Mussulman population ; but, on both sides,
goodwill and sympathy, a strict application of the principles of equality and justice, and severe measures against
all errors or excesses committed by the lower authorities.
In every instance, his Majesty the Sultan, the Ministers,
and the Governors of provinces have shown their firmness
in protecting the rights of the Israelites and in repairing
all acts of injustice and violence of which they might
have occasion to complain. The *Alliance* Committee at
Constantinople has never addressed itself in vain to the
Sultan to ask the reparation of an injustice or of a crime.
·   The Porte has associated itself in every way with the other
powers in all steps taken in favour of the Israelites of Roumania, and in 1877 it interceded in favour of the Servian
Jews in Constantinople. Last year, at the time of the fire
at Haskeuy, which so cruelly tried the Jews of that quarter,
the Sultan put himself at the head of a relief Committee,
and at the same time that he assisted the victims of the
calamity, he addressed the chief Rabbi of Constantinople
with sympathetic words for all the Israelites in Turkey.

The Law

If the Turkish Jews suffer it is not on account of the action of the Government against them. They have profited by all the liberal measures which have been created during 50 years and which inaugurated the famous hatti-sheriff of Gulhaneh of the 3rd November, 1839, completed by the hatti-humaiun of the 18th of February, 1856. The constitution of the 23rd December, 1876, proclaimed, by articles 17, 18, and 19, the equality of all Ottomans before the law and their admission to public functions. Three Jews took part in the Assembly of Deputies elected in 1877, and two were members of the Senate at the same time. Two others also occupied high positions in the Council of State.

Situation of the Israelites.

The evils under which the Turkish Israelites are suffering do not come from the legislation ; they are caused by the general state of the country, by its economical situation, by a want of organisation in the communities and the poverty and ignorance in which the despotic *regime* of former centuries have thrown them. The evil is deep-rooted and grave. The community of Constantinople, which embraces about 40,000 souls, has neither unity nor cohesion ; the education of the young has been neglected for centuries ; Jewish studies, which elsewhere have maintained the intellectual vitality of the Israelites, are here entirely abandoned or are transformed, as in Palestine, into purely mechanical exercises ; active and initiative men are wanting, misery has everywhere engendered lassitude, discouragement, the abandonment of general interests, and decadence. The elevation of this unhappy population is prepared by the schools which the *Alliance* has founded and by the liberal policy of the Government.

Protection accorded.—Punishment of outrages.

In Turkey in Europe and in Syria acts of violence towards the Jews on the part of the functionaries have become rare now that they know that the Government has decided to reprimand such acts. The sequestration of a young girl at Caiffa, in 1864 ; exactions on the part of the Governors of Larissa, Salonica, and Bagdad, in 1876; the troubles of Jannia, in 1872 ; of Smyrna, in 1873 ; of Tiria, in 1874 ; and the assassinations in Damascus about the same time, have always brought measures of reparation from the central power and the local authorities. The Government has even undertaken the protection of the poor communities of Diarbekir and Djarmuk, placed in the midst of the half-savage tribes of Kurdistan, over whom they exercise but a feeble authority. It also did what it could in 1873 to protect the communities of Yemen, and in 1875 it energetically maintained the municipal rights of the Israelites of Candia and authorisation to nominate a representative to the Council-General of this Island, and equally defended their rights at the elections of July 1881.

Blood Prejudice.

We known how tenacious still, among the Christian populations of the Orient, is the absurd and odious prejudice which is called the prejudice of blood, and which alleges that the Jews have need of Christian blood for the pretended mysteries of their Passover. Scarcely a year has passed in which this superstition has not been productive of trouble in the East among the Greeks and Armenians. We have seen it produced with its usual train of violence, riots, brutal confiscations and arbitrary arrests, at Adrianople, Larisa, Smyrna, and Marmora in 1872 ; at Cania, Kil-masti-Cassaba (near Brousse) in 1873 ; at Constantinople,

Vourla (near Smyrna), Adalia and Caratosch, in 1874; at Haskeui and Smyrna, in 1874; at Metelin and Kustendil, in 1880; at Kustendil, Aleppo and Melasso, in 1875; in 1884, again at Constantinople, in the environs of the Dardanelles, and at Tschorlou. The Central Committee and the Constantinople committee brought the best steps to bear on the Government for the purpose of putting an end to these troubles. The œcumenical Patriarchs of Constantinople have several times, on the demand of the Constantinople committee, issued encyclicals to the faithful destined to calm their minds and prevent these outbreaks, —touching proof on the part of the Greek clergy of their sentiments of humanity and fraternity!

Famine, War and Fire.

The Central Committee has several times furnished aid to the Israelites in Turkey. Could it abandon them in the painful trials to which they have had to submit? The limited subscriptions have enabled them to relieve the victims of the conflagrations, which broke out in the Couscoundjouk and Galata quarters at Constantinople in 1874, in that at Haskeui in 1883, and the victims of the earthquake in Chio, in 1881. During the famine which prevailed in provinces of Turkey in Asia in 1880, generous donors placed at the disposition of the *Alliance* the means of responding to the cry of distress from the communities in the remotest quarters of Asia : Diarbekir, Mossoul, Kerkouk, Ervil, Bashkala, had their share of the distributions, the same as Aleppo and Bagdad.

The War of 1877.

A great subscription, opened in 1877, at the time of the Russo-Turkish war, enabled help to be furnished to the cruelly-tried Israelites of Turkey in Europe. The war had driven them from their homes, and they wandered hither and thither without shelter or means of subsistence, flying before the invasion and bombardment of the towns, and the fury of the Bulgarians let loose against the Turks, who included in their reprisals everything that was not Christian. The scenes of devastation and murder at Kezanlik and Eski-Zagara, the destruction of the syna- gogues and pillage of the houses, will be well remembered. M. Veneziani, in the name of the *Alliance* and of Baron Hirsch, were the bearers of relief to their co-religionists. The work was long and difficult. Immediate repatriation would have been dangerous, and they were compelled to wait until the furious passions had been allayed. In Con- stantinople alone there were, yet in 1879, 1,320 refugees, and it is estimated that there were not less than 3,000 in the other Turkish towns. Little by little, they returned to their homes, and were assisted to resume their occupa- tions. At the commencement of 1880, the process of re- patriation was achieved.

Palestine.

The condition of the Israelites in Palestine is still inferior to that of their compatriots in Turkey in Europe. The legislation by which they are governed is the same, but Palestine is a poor country. The soil no longer possesses its ancient fertility ; arable land is rare ; there is a dearth of water everywhere ; there is not one trade route or cross- road ; industry and commerce are *nil* ; the apathy of the Christian and Jewish population is sustained by alms sent from abroad, which are no doubt indispensable, but which, if more judiciously employed, could be rendered of greater utility. The Jewish population, in particular, is enfee- bled by secular sufferings. It receives each year a consi- derable afflux of poor people—the old, infirm and widowed —from all parts of the earth seduced by the peculiar charm exercised over the imagination by Jerusalem, who would live by the *halucca*, and die in the Holy Land. Jerusalem, by their incessant influx, is transformed into a bottomless pit, in which, without any durable action or future utility, nearly two million francs are annually lost. A portion of this sum ought to be devoted to the foundation of permanent works of charity, schools, and professional works. The *halucca*, of which the necessity is recognised, would in no way suffer by it. The *Alliance* has commenced this work by founding professional and agricultural institutions at Jaffa and Jerusalem ; and the encouragement given by the public enables it to afford the necessary developments, and thus prepare the regeneration of Palestinian Judaism.

2. EGYPT.

The Jews of Egypt have no need of the co-operation of the *Alliance*. Egypt is, in certain respects, an European country, and they would sooner generously support than demand assistance of the work. The Central Committee could, and should, aid them in organising and developing their schools, which are already good.

It has aided the Alexandrian Israelites to fight against the prejudice of blood which from time to time has been aroused among the Greeks of Alexandria, and which occasioned a slight tumult in that town in 1880, a tumult which assumed graver proportions in 1881. A whole Jewish family was positively accused of having killed a Greek child, named Evangeli Fornaraki, whose body had been found in the sea. The Œcumenical Patriarch Joachim III wrote a touching letter on this subject to the late Dr. Moïse Allatini, the distinguished and regretted president of the Salonica Committee. Dr. Brouardel, of Paris, ably demonstrated in a medical journal the utter inanition of the

4

accusation. For the rest, they were able to rely upon the enlighten spirit of Greek justice before which the affair was investigated : the Tribunal of Corfu, after hearing the evidence for the prosecution, acquitted the accused.

At the south of Egypt, in Abyssinia, is a curious Jewish population. These are the Falashas, black Jews, diffused among the tribes, and who are chiefly engaged in agricultural pursuits, or as smiths, potters, weavers, masons, etc. Their number is estimated from 50,000 at 100,000 or at 200,000 souls. The *Alliance* sent out to them in 1867, Mr. Joseph Halévy, the well known learned. The observations made by Mr. Halévy on the Falashas were inserted in the Bulletin of the *Alliance* for the first semester of 1869. A complimentary version was subsequently issued by the Society of Hebrew Literature, and later the *Alliance,* in concert with the above Society, published a book in Ethiopian of the prayers of the Falasha Jews. These works have tended greatly to elucidate an historical problem of much interest.

3. Tunis and Tripoli.

In two countries relevant to Turkey, Tunis up to the establishment of the French Protectorate, and Tripoli, the Ottoman Government applied itself equally to the task of making preponderate the principles and sentiments with which it is animated. Thanks to its co-operation and that of the Consuls reparation was made in 1867, for the burning of a Synagogue at Zliten, the assassination of Saul Raccah at Tripoli. The sequestration of a young girl, a minor, at Bengazi, in 1868, equally called forth an action from the *Alliance.* When, in 1879, assassinations of Jews occurred at Zouvia and Tripoli, the intervention of the French and Italian Consuls obtained the condemnation of the culprits, who, in face of numerous precedents, seemed promised impunity.

The Bey of Tunis having accorded to his country in 1862 a liberal constitution of which the Jews should have profited, the *Alliance* hastened to thank him for the boon, which was, however, of short duration. The constitution could not be applied. In June, 1864, the tribes rebelled and fell upon the Jews at Nabel and the Island of Gerbi, who sought refuge in Tunis and Tripoli. The *Alliance* came to their relief with the aid of a subscription ; and thanks to the pressure of the European Governments an indemnity was afterwards awarded to the victims of this *émeute*. But it is difficult to protect Jews in a country agitated by anarchy, the insolence of the tribal chiefs and disobedience of functionaries : the Cadi of Derid could bestow the bastinado upon a Jew with impunity (1865) ; a nobleman did not scruple, in 1867, to imprison young Jewish girls in his castle for the purpose of converting them, who were, however, delivered by the French Consul. Murders of Jews became so frequent and numerous (17 were committed in 1868, and one at Tunis itself in January 1869), that they provoked an unanimous protest from the Consuls, addressed to the Bey on January 21, 1869. This time the murderers were pursued, acts of violence, instances of which were still to be had at Nabel in 1876, and at Doubdo in 1877, became more rare, until the French Protectorate finally put a stop to them altogether.

4. MOROCCO.

Altogether different to that in Turkey is the position of the Israelites in the two countries situated , so to speak, at the two extremities of the mussulman world : Morocco and Persia. The Jewish population of Morocco,

which originated partly from Spain and partly from the
Arabian countries, seems to have preserved more physical
and intellectual vigour than that of Turkey. It still has
learned Rabbis, Talmudic schools which have not entirely
degenerated, and shows proof of activity and energy. The
laws by which they are governed are deplorable. On the
coast the Jews are protected by the presence of the European ministers and consuls. In the interior they are the
prey of officials, the victims of the brigands who infest the
roads, and the scapegoat of a savage and fanatical population. They are subjected to taxes and humiliating drudgery,
and are beaten by that barbarous and murderous instrument of torture, the bastinado ; they are forbidden to
wear the turban or fez, and to ride on horseback ; in
Morocco itself, their women are forced to work daily, for a
ridiculous remuneration, on accoutrements for the army,
and keenly resent the shame of being exposed, unveiled,
to the gaze of the Arabs. They are held in contempt by
even the smallest Arab children, who pelt them with stones
and pull the clothes and beard of the Israelite rendered
venerable both by reason of his age and virtues.

This illused population is, nevertheless, active and
laborious, and maintains all the commerce between the
interior and the coast. The Emperor knows and appre-
ciates the services rendered by them to the country, but if
he does much to protect them, it does not depend entirely
upon him to change a situation which clings to the general
state and temper of the country.

Murders and Outrages.

The list of murders, outbreaks, extortions, and acts of
violence in regard to which the *Alliance* has been invoked,
and has succeeded by its entreaties in moving the European
ministers and obtaining their interference, is long. It

comprises the assassinations at Larache, the violences of
the Cadi of Demnat, violences which are repeated even
to-day in the same locality, in 1864 ; the arbitrary impri-
sonment of the Jewish Junta at Tetuan, in 1865 ; in 1866
and 1867, the assassinations at Saffi and Tetuan, and the
siege of Tetuan by a brigand named Aissa and his band,
who held in terror the Jews of the town ; the fresh
murders committed at Saffi in 1868 ; the Jews of Rabbat,
compelled to put salt on the heads of criminals on Satur-
days, in 1872 ; the order prohibiting the Jews of Saffi,
Morocco and Mazagan to dress like Europeans ; and the
condemnation to five hundred strokes of a cane of an
Israelite of Fez for having committed, on the order of a
doctor, the crime of entering a Mussulman bath, in 1873 ;
the assassinations at Saffi in 1874 ; at Larache in 1877 ;
the disturbances which followed the news of the death of
the Sultan, in 1878 ; the atrocious scenes of cruelty which
occurred at Morocco and Entifa (near Morocco), in 1880 ;
and, lastly, the strenuous efforts made by Morocco, in the
same year, to abolish the Protections, and deprive the
Jews of a guarantee as efficacious as necessary.

Protectionist measures and Firmans.

In a country where the will of the sheriff is sovereign, the
firmans of the Emperor are the sole legal protection of the
Israelites. A firman obtained in February, 1864, by Sir
Moses Montefiore, whom the persecutions of 1863 had called to that country, assured to the Jews the good-will of
the Emperor, permitted them to be treated like all other
subjects, and exempted them from the laws of exception and
above all bastinado. This firman was renewed at the
instance of the Governments in August 1872, and again on
the advent of the new Sultan in the spring of 1874. But if
these firmans are an evident proof of the good inclinations

of the Sultans, and a legal instrument of serious value, their efficacy is doubtful. It was the European ministers who in 1864, by a collective step, obtained the deposition of the Governor of Demnat, and the release of the Israelites of Tetuan. It was a demonstration of the coast effected by a French frigate which also brought punishment to the brigand Aïssa, on May 13, 1868. To the same protection must be attributed the repression ot the assassinations at Saffi in 1868, and the renewal of the decrees of 1864. Every year, on the occasion of their visit to the Sultan, the European Ministers reminded him of the necessity of protecting the Jews. The Central Committee has never failed, when necessary, to recommend this question to them, and in January 1866 and June 1876 entered into direct relations for this purpose with the Extraordinary Embassies sent to Paris from Morocco.

The Protections.

The Moorish Jews found another guarantee in what are known as the *Protections*. The majority of the European Powers have a number of indigenous and foreign *protégés* at Morocco, who, in consequence of these Protections, are exempt from native jurisdictions, and subject only to that of their Consuls. The Protections, as far as France is concerned, are established at Morocco by the Treaty and Convention of 1767 and August 19, 1863. Morocco greatly desires their abolition, and on February 8, 1880, declared that it no longer recognised them. This measure excited among the Israelites the most lively emotion.

The Conference at Madrid.

There were 563 *protégés* at Morocco at this epoch, of which 103 were Israelites, but the scope of the Protections must not be calculated after their numerical importance.

They are a barrier against the acts of violence and exactions of the authorities. The 103 franchised Jews of
Morocco are the nucleus and basis of support of all Moorish
Judaism. In a Memorandum addressed by the *Alliance* to
the European Governments it was shown to what extent
the Protections were indispensable. A list of 307 Israelites
assassinated within a period of three years, (1864 to 1866)
in one part of Morocco only, and leaving about 1,200
widows and orphans, sufficiently demonstrated what would
be their condition were the Protections to be abolished.
Mr. Charles Netter and Mr. E. F. Veneziani, delegates of
the Central Committee, proceeded to Madrid for the purpose of upholding these views before the members of the
Conference. The resolution of France and Italy being
unshaken, the Powers ended by adopting their opinion of the
question and the Protections were maintained. The Conference commenced on May 19, 1880, and accomplished its
work by the end of the month of June. It did not confine
itself to upholding the rights of the *protégés*, but addressed
a demand to the Sultan in favour of religious liberty for the
Jews and Christians. The Moorish Government responded
to the demand of the Powers by a Note on September 18,
1880, assuring them that it accorded full liberty to both
Christians and Jews.

Aid.

The Jews of Morocco are poor. The *régime* under which
they exist has reduced them to destitution, and the quarters
mellahs) in which they are imprisoned present a lamentable aspect. The slightest epidemic makes frightful
ravages, and in years of dearth their sufferings are most
cruel.

The *Alliance* has more than once assisted these communities to cleanse and purify the Jewish quarter, and principally, in 1865, it was able to obtain from several persons

an important subscription for the amelioration of the mellah of Mogador. At the time of the famine of 1868 an extensive subscription was made in their favour, and in favour of the Israelites of Tunis and Palestine, and help was also sent at the time of the typhus and famine of 1878. There is no other population more worthy of these proofs of sympathy !

5. PERSIA

The Situation.

In Persia the position of the Israelites is lamentable. Their sufferings are in no way attenuated by the proximity of European countries and the immediate action of Western civilization. Exactions and violences are incessant, and remain unnoticed. The Jews are forced to cringe to the Mussulmans. They must dress in a particular manner. The murderer of a Jew can escape from the affair by a pecuniary arrangement. It suffices on the most trifling testimony for a Jew to be accused of blasphemy, to place his life and the lives of his coreligionists in jeopardy. Forced conversions are innumerable, and the convert is the sole inheritor of the patrimony of the family. At the market, the Jews are obliged to wait until the Mussulmans have finished in order to make their purchases; if they chance to touch a fruit, it is contaminated, and they are forced to buy it ; on rainy days they are compelled to remain indoors, because the religious impurity of the Jew would be conducted by the rain water to the Mussulman. A special tax is collected, under the name of the tax of the Jews. The communities are held conjointly responsible for their impost and cannot consent to the departure of any of their members. This is how the poor Jews are treated in the towns where their communities formerly flourished, and

which have kept alive the remembrance of Esther and
Mardocai.

H. M. the Shah in Europe.

The proceedings of the Central Committee have never
ceased to find the best reception at the Persian Embassy
in Paris and London. The Governments of France and
England have often pressed the complaints of the Jews
coming from Teheran, Hamadan and other localities. When,
in 1867, on the occasion of the disappearance of a young
Mussulman girl at Balforusch 18 Jews were massacred, the
united efforts of the English and French Governments
and the Persian Embassy in Paris obtained the reparation
demanded by justice. A great manifestation was prepared
in connexion with the journey of the Shah in 1873: All
the Committees of the *Alliance* in the large towns at which
he alighted, proceeded to offer him homage, and bore to
him their wishes in regard to their coreligionists. He
received addresses from the Committees of the *Alliance* of
Berlin, Amsterdam and Brussels at the beginning of June,
1873 ; that of the Anglo-Jewish Association about the end
of the same month ; and then successively the addresses
of the Israelites of Rome, Vienna and Constantinople.

At Paris, the Minister Houssein Khan signed, on
July 13, 1873, with the assent of the Shah, an official
report of the visit of the *Alliance* which contained most
reassuring promises for the situation of the Israelites,
among others that to protect any schools the *Alliance* might
subsequently found in the country.

These representations were not without influence on the
condition of the Israelites of Persia, and it can be safely
affirmed that they have left a lasting impression on the
mind of the Sovereign. In april 1876, an outbreak against
the Jews of Hamadan, in whose quarter the body of a

woman had been found, was promptly suppressed; and in the preceding year a telegram from the president of the *Alliance* to Hussein Khan was sufficient to obtain the punishment, at Hamadan, of the malefactors who had burnt alive a Jew accused of blasphemy and pillaged the Jewish houses.

A young Israelite of the country, adopted, in the first place, by the Anglo Jewish Association, is now actually in the school of the *Alliance* at Paris, preparing himself for the purpose of proceeding out there in the capacity of schoolmaster. The Israelites of Persia are plunged in the greatest ignorance. They have neither schools nor books of any kind, and are cut off from the entire world. The instruction the *Alliance* could bring would be of immense importance to them.

IV.

SCHOOLS, APPRENTICESHIP, SCIENTIFIC WORK

1. PRIMARY SCHOOLS AND APPRENTICESHIP.

Aim of the Schools.

At the same time that the *Alliance* helps the persecuted Israelites, it works for their intellectual and moral improvement. The schools are its work of predilection, and in them it concentrates nearly all its resources and a great part of its efforts.

Extension of the Schools.

The schools of the *Alliance* are to-day established along the coast of the Mediterranean, from Tangiers to Tunis, from Smyrna to Caïffa and Beyrouth, from Salonica to the Dardanelles and Constantinople; they spread over Turkey, Bulgaria, and Roumelia; enter Asia as far as Bagdad; advance, in Turkey in Europe, to the end of the Balkans and to the extreme northern coasts of the Black Sea; penetrate to Morocco, in the heart of the country, and as far as the town of Fez. The day will come, it is to be hoped, when they will find their way into Russia, Roumania, and Servia, and even Persia.

Utility of the Schools.

Everywhere the *Alliance* founds a scholastic establishment, it brings some rays of Western civilisation. The benefits of the instruction cannot be described, they can only be seen and felt. The children, formerly brought up in the narrow and unwholesome *Talmud-Toras*, by masters whose only art consists in chanting and mechanically translating prayers, are placed, in the schools of the *Alliance*, under the direction of professors formed by the Society under modern methods, and who give an instruction as solid as it is varied. The moral effect of this teaching, so new in these countries, will soon manifest itself. The Israelite youth acquires habits of order and cleanliness, the children acquire the sentiment of personal dignity, the character is raised, the intelligence opens and expands. They learn the language, the history, and the geography of their country. The *Alliance* has placed these matters at the head of its programme; they learn a European language which permits them to go to the source of Western literature and to read our elementary books of science, history and travels. A whole world of ideas and new sentiments is revealed to them and creates quite a stir in that poor Jewish quarter of which the horizon until now had been so narrow. It is truly a resurrection.

Moral Results.

The action of the school has already made itself felt in the generations who have reaped the benefit of it. In a large number of towns, as in Aleppo, Constantinople, Rustchuk, Smyrna, and elsewhere, the late scholars have formed little reading classes where they continue to instruct themselves, and they also contribute pecuniarily to the school. The parents, converted by the children, show a less narrow mind; they read the Jewish and political papers. Everywhere, in fact, the establishment of schools by the *Alliance* has inspired in the native populations a sentiment of respect for the Jews. They despised them before, now they esteem them and take them for their model. Christian or other schools are created after the model of those of the *Alliance*, and sometimes with the help of its professors. Since the foundation of the schools the Central

Committee has liberally opened them to children of all religions. Every father of a family, no matter what his religion, can send his son and he will be received with eagerness. Catholic, Grecian, Mussulman, European, Oriental Turkish, and Armenian children sit on the same forms, and precious friendly relations are thus established between them.

Material Results.

The material results obtained by the schools are not less satisfactory. Besides the general education which is given to the children, they acquire practical knowledge of the greatest utility. The sorrowful economic situation of the Israelites in uncivilised countries is, without doubt, due to permanent causes over which it is difficult to triumph. In general, however, it is remarked that the Israelites of the commercial classes have, thanks to the instruction of their children, greater facilities in their foreign relations; they undertake operations with countries which they did not know before ; and their children will occupy places or found establishments in far-off countries. Children well endowed, on leaving school, are often admitted in consulates or in public or private administrations. Others, finding themselves provided with a trade, emigrate to countries less unhappy than their own. The school at Bagdad numbers pupils to-day established at Bassora, Bombay, Hong-Kong, King-Foo, London, and Manchester; the schools of Tangiers and Tetuan are sending their pupils to Algeria, Spain, Italy, Marseilles, London, and even as far as Brazil.

History of the Schools.

The work of the schools, which to-day is so greatly developed, had a humble commencement, resources were wanting, and to-day even they are far below the demand. Much has been done, but much more remains to be done.

The Society hardly existed, the first penny of which it was able to dispose was consecrated to the school at Tetuan, each new receipt being immediately consecrated to a new school. The boys' school at Tangiers dates from 1864 ; the first school established in Turkey in Asia was that of Bagdad, in 1865 ; with that of Adrianople, in 1867, the scholastic map of the *Alliance* was extended to Turkey in Europe ; and the first school in Tunis dates from 1878. The town of Constantinople, the extraordinary extent of which, the scattering of the Jewish population in the different quarters and in the furthest faubourgs, the dearness of living, and the absence of all organisation in the Jewish community, presented to the creation of schools extraordinary difficulties, which were only surmounted in 1874, after the magnificent donation almost specially made for that object by Baron de Hirsch. The most important schools in Bulgaria and Roumelia were established after the last war. Last, the opening of a school at Jerusalem, which was regarded as next to impossible, was accomplished without the least obstacle and with the greatest success in 1882. It is altogether due to the exceptional concurrence lent to this work by the Montagu Committee, of London, and to the activity, wisdom, and tact of the director. The school at Fez, with which the *Alliance* has penetrated to the interior of Morocco, dates from 1883.

Girls' Schools.

A great improvement was accomplished in the work of the schools when the *Alliance*, after having founded boys' schools, was able to occupy itself in creating schools for girls. In the East more than anywhere else the raising of the woman by instruction and the development of her authority in the family are appealed to in order to exercise the most happy influence over the education of the children. The future mother brought up in the schools of the *Alliance* learns to keep her household more regular and to do needle-work so necessary for the good order of the house ; she contracts habits of order and cleanliness which render the inside of the house more agreable and permits her, by the new part which she will fulfil in the family, to take her legitimate place in the intellectual and moral direction of the children. By the instruction which she herself will have received she will be prepared to note the effects of their instruction, to judge of their progress, and to help them forward in the way of culture and civilisation. For the *Alliance* she will be the most active and the most precious auxiliary.

Apprenticeship of the Boys.

The work of apprenticeship is the necessary completion of the school. When the child has finished his round of the classes, it often happens that he does not know how to employ the knowledge which he has acquired, thus running the risk of again falling into vagabondage or the miserable industry of the hawker. The *Alliance*, in teaching him a trade, gives a direction to his activity and a guide to his good will ; it teaches him to live by the fruit of his labour and prepares for him an honorable future. In the Eastern and African towns, where there is no commerce at all and agriculture, in the actual state of things, is inaccessible to the Jews, the future of the Israelites lies in the exercise of manual labour. Everywhere they have received with eagerness the foundation of works destined to spread the practice of trades. The *Alliance* some time ago created such establishments at Bagdad, Tangiers, and Tetuan ; an important annual subvention from Baron de Hirsch permitting the Society, since 1878, to considerably augment the number. It is not apprentices which are wanted, but masters. In many towns, it is stated with the most lively regret that non-Jewish masters refuse to take Jewish apprentices, and it is often impossible to over-come their resistance.

Apprenticeship of Young Girls.

The committee has extended to young girls the benefits of a professional education, and Baron de Hirsch willingly accorded his generous help for this new work, which commenced its functions in 1884. It is not possible to place young girls as apprentices to board with the masters, such a measure presents inconveniences of more than one kind; another organisation, therefore, became necessary. The Central Committee decided then to create, side by side with the girls' schools where the scholars were taught needlework, workshops for the making of women's clothes, linen, embroidery, as well as for ironing and weaving. These workshops are directed by mistresses specially engaged for that object. They already exist in Adrianople, Constantinople, Damascus, Rustchuk, and Smyrna, and the Committee is considering means of founding more in other towns. This work responds to a veritable want and is expected to be of great service ; it will raise the Jewish woman and will contribute to relieve the poverty of the Jewish population.

Importance of the Schools.

The value and importance of these institutions appear from the following numbers.

They embrace a scholastic population of more than 9,000 children, of which there are 8,800 pupils (6,200 boys, 2,600 girls) and about 500 apprentices.

The number of professors engaged by the *Alliance* is 92.

The total number of teachers is 304.

The annual amount of the subventions of the *Alliance* is nearly 325,000 fr.

Institutions (schools, apprenticeship works for boys, girls' workshops) are established in the following localities:

Aleppo (Turkey in Asia), boys, apprenticeship for boys ; Adrianople (Turkey in Europe), boys, girls, apprenticeship for boys.

Bagdad (Turkey in Asia), boys, apprenticeship for boys; Beyrouth (Turkey in Asia), boys, girls.

Caïffa (Turkey in Asia), boys ; Choumla (Bulgaria), boys, girls, apprenticeship for boys ; Constantinople (Turkey in Europe), 7 boys' schools, 5 girls' schools, apprenticeship for boys, girls workshops.

Damascus (Turkey in Asia), boys, girls, girls workshop ; Dardanelles (Turkey in Europe), boys, apprenticeship for boys.

Fez (Morocco), boys.

Jerusalem (Turkey in Asia), boys and boys' workshop.

Mehdia (Tunis), boys.

Philippopolis (Roumelia), boys, apprenticeship for boys.

Rustchuk (Bulgaria), boys, girls, apprenticeship for boys, girls workshop.

Salonica (Turkey in Europe), boys, girls, apprenticeship for boys ; Samacoff (Bulgaria), boys, apprenticeship for boys ; Smyrna (Turkey in Asia), boys, girls, apprenticeship for boys, girls workshop ; Sofia (Bulgaria), boys, girls; Sousse (Tunisia), boys.

Tangiers (Morocco), boys, girls, apprenticeship for boys; Tatar-Bazardjik (Roumelia), boys, girls, apprenticeship for boys ; Tetuan (Morocco), boys, girls, apprenticeship for boys; Tunis, boys, girls, apprenticeship for boys.

Varna (Bulgaria), boys.

Widdin (Bulgaria), boys.

Yamboli (Roumelia), boys.

The total amount of the annual expenses, part of which is furnished by the communities, exceeds 680,000 fr.

It is a great satisfaction to the Central Committee to see the important assistance lent to the work by the communities, and it is touching to see them, in the midst of their poverty and misery, imposing such heavy sacrifices upon themselves for the education of their children. The *Alliance* has adopted the rule of only assisting those who are ready to assist themselves ; they must prove, by their

5

contributions, the interest they take in instruction. The local committees must concur in the work by the financial administration of the schools and workshops, the inspection of the apprentices, and by the moral support given to the directors.

School Houses.

These are ordinarily at the charge of the community, the *Alliance* making it a rule not to furnish school houses nor to contribute to their reparation. However, thanks to the liberality of a certain number of donors, especially that of Baron de Hirsch and Mr. S.-H. Goldschmidt, the Society is the proprietor of several houses at Constantinople-Balata; Constantinople-Haskeuy, the Dardanelles, Philippopolis, Rustchuk, Salonica, Smyrna, and Tunis.

Scholastic Material.

For two or three years the *Alliance* has made great efforts to furnish all the schools with maps, globes, and cabinets of physic. Each school has a library for the use of the professors which is very varied, and there is also a reading library containing about 300 volumes, and which is continually being increased, for the use of the scholars, apprentices, late pupils, and in short for the use of every one in the town who wishes to take advantage of it.

The Talmud-Toras.

The number of scholars in the schools of the *Alliance* could be easily increased. The number is nearly 9,000, and could be 50,000 or more, if the Committee would take charge of the *Talmud-Toras*, or if its resources would permit it to do so.

Much has been said concerning the small value of these institutions, the teaching therein being next to worthless. It is, however, to these schools, which defend tradition, the force of habit, the power of personal interest, that the

Jewish communities still confide the larger number of their children, and consecrate, in the form of expenses for clothes and nourishment, of entertainments and pensions to the Rabbis, the greater part of their resources. It has often been a question of fusing these schools with the Society's schools, which fusion would be a great progression, but it is impossible to accomplish it at present.

It would give the *Alliance* a considerable number of new pupils, but it would demand new and larger school houses, a staff ten times more numerous, resources incomparably greater for board and the furnishing of material, and, lastly, a certain progress in the mind of the communities, who actually regard the disappearance of these ancient institutions with vexation. The school at Tunis is an exception. Since its very foundation it has absorbed all the other schools in the town or rendered them superfluous; this school has been, from the first day, a grand institution comprising more than 800 pupils, the largest scholastic establishment, the most prosperous, and, perhaps, the finest on the African coast (1).

The School at Jerusalem.

The school at Jerusalem is equally worthy of a separate place in the scholastic institutions of the *Alliance* for its special organisation and the interest which attaches to it. Here it was impossible to ask for the pecuniary help of the community ; the Society was obliged to support all the expenses and feed and clothe the pupils besides. This institution costs about 34,500 fr. per annum, a large portion of which is furnished by the Montagu Committee, of London; Messrs. de Rothschild Brothers, of Paris ; Baron de Hirsch , for apprenticing the children ; and by the Relief Funds for the Russian Jews at the London Mansion-

---

1, This school received a prize at Amsterdam Exposition of 1883.

House. In this great institution the school is intimately associated with the work of apprenticeship. The latter comprises six workshops : a joiner's, an upholsterer's, a forge, a turner's, a tailor's, a shoemaker's, and lastly a workshop for day work. The Anglo-Jewish Association proposes to send at its own cost a master mechanician. The institution comprises in all 125 pupils, of which there are 63 apprentices. The activity displayed in the workshops is astonishing, all those who visit them being struck with the spirit which is shown and the ardour of the children. The products being absorbed by the town, the school has become the furnisher of all the inhabitants. It is a laborious hive which serves as an example of activity and work to the whole population of Jerusalem.

Preparatory Schools.

This collection of scholastic establishments is completed by the Preparatory schools in Paris and the Agricultural school at Jaffa.

The Preparatory boys' school is destined to create professors for the primary schools. Founded in Paris in 1868, it received from the French Government the judicial personallity by a decree of the 12th February, 1880. It counts, on the average, 24 pupils, divided into four classes. The pupils are selected every year from among the best scholars of the primary schools of the *Alliance*, and, their instruction finished, they are placed, first, as assistants in the schools, then, as their experience increases, as directors. The governesses of the *Alliance* are procured in the same manner, and are brought up in the excellent school founded in Paris by a donation from the late L.-R. Bischoffsheim which willingly receives the pupils of the Society. The formation of governesses for the Society's schools began in 1873 ; the average number of pupils is 12, and the annual expense from 12,000 to 14,000 francs. Owing to this measure, the *Alliance* possesses a body of professors specially prepared for the mission which is confided to them, knowing beforehand the country in which they may be called upon to exercise it and the most proper way to act towards the children and their parent. Here they succeed, where a European professor might fail.. Their task is always laborious, sometimes difficult, but they fulfil it with as much intelligence as devotion.

2. The Agricultural School of Jaffa.

History of its Foundation.

The creation of this school is solely due to the initiative and energy of the late Charles Netter, member of the Central Committee, who consecrated, with an absolute disinterestedness, several years of his life to its creation. Having lived many years in the East, and being thoroughly acquainted with the Jewish populations of those regions, its wants, and its sufferings, Charles Netter found himself deeply touched by such an amount of misery, and he conceived the hope of being able to regenerate the Judaism of Palestine by founding in that country an agricultural school. All the persons who put interest to that unfortunate country are unanimous in declaring that the safety and security of the Jewish population could only be brought about by agriculture. But a common error existed in the belief that it sufficed simply to furnish them with land to cure the evil. It is an illusion which still weighs heavily on all the projects lately formed for the good for the Israelites of Palestine and other countries. If it requires an apprenticeship of many years to make an artisan, it requires a still greater number to form agriculturists ; you cannot improvise them from one day to

another, as many persons seem to imagine. Charles Netter
started from the idea—a very just one—that you could never have in Palestine good Israelitish agriculturists without
giving an appropriate education to the new generations
when young. He submitted to the Central Committee,
in 1868, a project to found at Jaffa, not an agricultural
colony, but, what was quite different, an Agricultural
School for the purpose of instructing a certain number of
children taken specially from Jerusalem and destined to
become the nucleus of an Israelitish agricultural population
in Palestine. This institution, in the idea of the founder,
should bring about the salvation of the Israelites in
Palestine.

Charles Netter at Jaffa.

Without absolutely indulging in all the hopes indulged
in by Charles Netter, the Central Committee thought it
would be worthy of the *Alliance*, worthy of the Jewish
society, to attempt to bring about this grand and difficult
enterprise. Regenerate poor Palestine by labour, revive
agriculture in a country where formerly Jewish agriculture
was fecund and amongst a population which a spirit of
persecution had long estranged from this kind of labour,
was assuredly an important work, which responded to a
general wish. The Central Committee adopted the plan
which Charles Netter had conceived, and undertook the
execution.

Charles Netter started for Constantinople in August,
1869, thence to Jaffa. On the 5th of April, 1870, he
obtained an Imperial firman by which the Government of
the Porte leased to the *Alliance*, for an indefinite period,
2,600 mesures (about 240 hectares) a splendid piece of
land situated in the neighbourhood of the town of Jaffa,
on payment of an annual impost of 7,500 piastres, with
exemption of this farming during the first ten years,

including several other favours which certainly bore witness to the sympathy of the. Government for the enterprise. Charles Netter applied himself immediately to the work ; he marked the boundaries of the land accorded by his Majesty the Sultan, and dug the trenches which marked the frontier. The preliminary works, aided by a subscription which produced a sum of 16,000 fr., fell off during the war 1870-1871. Wanting in resources, Mr. S.-H. Goldschmidt twice made to the *Alliance*, in 1870 and 1871, a donation of 50,000 fr. By degrees, a habitable house was constructed, and Charles Netter, who, up to that moment, had been living in the trenches he had formed, was enabled to take possession of a comfortable chamber; 25,000 stocks of vine-trees were planted, a part of the land was set out for a garden, and another portion set apart for the peasants. Pupils were admitted, at the origin to the number of 20, at present there are 30 at least ; a *chef* for the purposes of culture was engaged, as well as a master gardener ; strawberry trees, asparagus, orange trees were planted; vast plots of ground for gardening, wells and canals constructed ; instruments of husbandry, besides beasts of burden were purchased.

First State of the School.

Mr. S. H. Goldschmidt, who went to visit the school in 1873, writes in these terms to the Anglo-Jewish Association :

I was agreeably surprised at the beautiful situation of our property. It is about forty-five minutes'walk from the town of Jaffa, in following the grand route of Jerusalem, which traverses it directly in length about 1,500 metres.

In the lower part the soil is everywhere good, with the exception of a large space, which is rather sandy, planted with pine trees; the hills are of a rocky formation, but Mr. Netter thinks that vine trees may be easily planted.

When I passed through, about the middle of April, the barley was ripe, the wheat in flower, both promising a rich harvest, and the crop fully came up to my previsions. The cultivation is done in part by ourselves, and in part by the Arabs, who pay a quit rent of 35 per cent. on the raw production. Our products are much superior to those of the Arabs; I made a comparison of our ears of corn and theirs, and I found that ours contained twice as many grains, and much larger. For the moment this evident superiority hardly compensates us for the sums of money we have expended in the culture in the absence of an experienced agriculturist.

If at first it was thought that a domain of 240 hectares could be rendered sufficiently productive to meet the wants of an establishment for instruction of the importance which an agricultural school should have, it was a decided error ; such is not true in a general sense, and still less so in the particular situation in which we found ourselves. In France, it must be a splendid farm which will give 100 fr. of revenue per hectare, and furthermore it must be a real farm, with buildings, roads, a soil well improved, and a rolling capital of £ 6,000 or £ 8,000 sterling. What the Government has given us is not a farm, but 240 hectares of uncultivated ground, covered with useless herbage. To render this land productive it will be necessary, for several years during its cultivation, to make considerable advances in money for the construction of buildings and roads, for the manuring and improvement of the soil, and, furthermore, a rolling capital, and a man of experience to direct the farm. Nothing of this kind was at the disposal of Mr. Netter, but he had the courage to march forward without capital, confident in his final success. A certain amount of capital was found, but the sum-total of the expenses up to the present day are about £ 6,000 sterling (150,000 fr.). The buildings exist, roads of considerable length have been constructed and trenches dug; the soil has been cleansed, and put in a proper state for cultivation, several trees have been planted, a choice collection of cattle, workmen's tools and implements, and, what is better still, a great amount of technical experience generally has been acquired. This experience has shown that an institution of this kind will never be at one and the same time a duly-installed farm to be speculated upon with the sole view of the benefits to be reaped therefrom ; there is a building for educa tional purposes, which at all time requires the supervision of the director, with the aid of professors and other employés, and where the cultivation of a part of the soil with a view to a knowledge of agricultural instruction must be utilised, as every good farmer should do.

I do not despair of seeing, at the end of a few years, the above institution capable of meeting its own wants, when we shall be in a position to come to its aid, and when we can dispose of a certain number of young men arrived at man's estate, whose intelligence, as regards work, will be not only profitable but remunerative, and when we shall be able to cultivate scientifically this soil so fertile and which is blessed with such a fine climate.

Progress of the School.

Great efforts have been and are still necessary to give to the Agricultural School its full development ; above all, for the formation of technical staff necessary for its growth. Serious progress has, nevertheless, been accomplished since, owing to the sacrifices which the *Alliance* has imposed upon itself.

Very important constructions and plantations were undertaken in 1875, in the repairs of routes and trenches, construction of new rooms, a basin, a well, the cleansing of 8,000 square yards for the formation of a second garden adjoining the first one of 20,000 square yards, planted with fresh vine trees. A further donation by Mr. Goldschmidt of a sum of 22,000 fr., paid in 1874 and 1875, tended to facilitate the works. Even at the present moment divers constructions are being executed at the expense of the same donor, who expressed the wish to open for the purpose a credit of 21,000 fr.

At the end of 1875 the number of square yards of ground cleansed for making gardens was 50,000, and 1,000 lemon trees were planted. The works necessary for making a third garden were commenced in 1876. It results from a report sent during the first semester of 1876 that the school contained at that epoch :

In open ground, lemon trees, orange trees, cedars, plum-'rees, peaches, pear trees, apple trees, quince trees, etc 4.746
In the nursery gardens, trees of the same sort 2.424
Plants for the purpose of placing in the nursery gardens (acacias, mulberry trees, palm trees, walnut trees, cherry trees, etc.). 5.320
In the orchard and nursery garden combined, including almond and apricot trees 5.300
Vine trees planted and to be planted 4.000
Trees in the avenues and alleys. 3.398
Superficies of cleansed ground, 55,075 square yards.

Charles Netter, who had come back from Europe, returned to Jaffa in 1877, for the purpose of installing a new director ; he went for the last time in February, 1881, after the fatigues of his sojourn at Brody. It was there, in the very institution which was his work, that he died, suddenly snatched from his family, from his friends, from the *Alliance*, completely borne down by an overwhelming burden. It was there that the modest monument of the *Alliance* was raised to his memory !

Actual State of the School.

The following is a description of the School as furnished by Mr. E. F. Veneziani, member of the Central Committee, who visited the establishment in 1883 : —

The whole of the left wing, with its annexes at the extreme end, formerly constructed, and comprising the residence of the Director, the sleeping rooms, the kitchen, the refectory, and the magazines, have undergone repairs.

The right wing comprising the school-house and the oratory, the forge, and the magazines, have been enlarged ; the roofing has also been repaired.

Several new rooms are being constructed at this moment and are being parcelled out.

The School is engaged in the manufacture of white wine, which is likely to turn out a good commercial product. All that is wanting is a good cellar for its preservation, and one is now being constructed in a rock 20 metres in length and five metres in width.

The annexes comprise the stables and pigeon-houses, a carpenter's shop', a washhouse, a bakehouse, a distillery, workmen's habitations, three wells, and three reservoirs. Works have also been commenced for the sinking of an artesian well.

The material is composed of ploughs, tumbrils, harrows, wine-presses, machines for thrashing wheat, etc.

The horned cattle comprises 20 oxen, about 150 sheeps, two horses, ten mules, pigeons, fowls, etc.

The wines are prosperous, and there is reason to hope for good results.

The orange plantations, the lemon trees, the pomegranate, the mulberry trees, etc., produce fruit in abundance, but the cultivation still leaves much to be desired. In 1883 the school sold 150,000 oranges.

The 1,700 plants of young cedars for the production of *etrogim* have not yet given very satisfactory results, owing to the gardener not possessing the necessary experience.

The number of pupils is from 30 to 33, without counting the Russian children received into the school in 1881, and, by degrees, were handed over to their parents living in America.

The greater part of the pupils work in the garden, but some of them devote themselves exclusively to the different trades taught in the school. They are divided as follows : twenty gardeners, three wine-growers, two carpenters, two turners, one blacksmith, and one tailor. There are some pupils yet too young to receive a professional instruction.

The actual *personnel* is composed of a Director, two assistants, a steward, a gardener, and a head wine-grower.

The nursery garden is the unique of its kind situated on the Syrian side; it furnishes all the plants which are required for the country.

The importance and the magnitude of this work strikes the eye at once ; its utility is incontestable. It has had to struggle with numerous difficulties, emanating, on the one side, from local conditions, and on the other, from the inexperience of the Central Committee and the persons charged to direct the institution. Everything was new in this country for the most experienced agriculturists, added to unfavourable circumstances. It is to be hoped that in a few years from hence this school, favoured by the considerable resources which are necessary to ensure its success, will respond to the hopes indulged in by its much regretted founder and the vows breathed forth by all the friends of the Holy Land!

3. Scientific Work.

At the same time that it gave an impetus to primary instruction, the *Alliance* sought to contribute to the progress of the Jewish science.

Prizes.

The *Alliance* began its action by founding prizes for any given subject. One of these subjects gave rise to the production of a work by Mr. Elie Benamozegh, of Livourne, published under the title " La Morale Juive ". But very soon after, enlightened by its proper experience and that of all the learned bodies, the *Alliance* plainly saw that the process did not furnish to results aimed at. The promise of a prize never succeeds in turning aside learned men from the course of their studies; a scientific work should be spontaneous. The *Alliance* at the present day is satisfied with encouraging the publication of learned works and the acquisition of the greatest number of copies. All original scientific works are certain of the support of the Central Committee.

Subventions.

Here is the list of the most important publications subventioned by the *Alliance*:

Elie Benamozegh, *Morale juive et morale chrétienne;* Paris, 1867. — A. Berliner, *Targum Onkelos*; 2 vol.; Berlin, 1884. —

ope

M. Bloch, *Takkanot, die Institutionen des Judenthums*; Przemyz] 1884.—Commentary on Jeremias by Rabbi Josef ben Simeon Kara, published by Léon Schlosberg; Paris, 1881.—*Commentaries on the later Prophets by R. Eleazar of Beaugenci, l. Isaiah*; Londres, 1879.—*Commentarium quem in Pentateuchum comrosuit R. Samuel ben Meir*, published by D. Rosin; Breslau, 1881. — *A Commentary on the book of Proverbs attributed to Abraham ibn Ez'u*, published by S. R. Driver, Oxford, 1880.—*Dikduke hasoferim, variæ lectiones in Mischnam et in Talmud babylonicum*, published by R. Rabbinowiz; Munich. 1867-79. — *Dikduke hat'amim des Ahron ben Mosche ben Ascher*, published by S. Baer and H. L. Strack; Leipzig, 1879. — S. Frensdorf, *Die Massora Magna*; Hanovre, 1876. — M. Friedlænder, *Patristische und talmudische Studien;* Wien, 1878. — Corrado Guidetti, *Pro Judæis, reflessioni e documenti;* Turin, 1884. — Jacob Hamburger, *Real-Encyclopædie für Bibel und Talmud*; Strelitz, 1866-1878.—Scientific Journals: *Bet Talmud*, by Weiss and Friedmann, of Vienne; *Letterbode*, of Roest, of Amsterdam; *Monat·schr·ft*, by Frankel-Graetz; *Magasin*, of Berliner and Hoffmann, of Berlin; *Revue des Etudes juives*, of the Société des Etudes juives, of Paris.—Isidor Kaim, *Ein Jahrhundert der Judenemancipation;* Leipzig, 1869. — Dr A. Kohut, *Aruch completum*; Vienne,1880-82. — J. Levy, *Neuhebræisches und chaldæisches Wærtebuch*; Leipzig, 1879. — L. Læwenstein, *Geschichte der Juden am Bodensee und Umgebung;* Constance, 1879.—S. D. Luzzatto's, *Hebræische Briefe;* Przemyzl, 1882. — *Rabbi Mosis Maimonidis liber More Nebuchim a rabbi Jehuda Alcharisi in linguam hebræam translatus;* Londres, 1879. — *Masechet Soferim, der talmudische Tractat der Schreiber*, published by Dr Joel Müller; Leipzig, 1878. — Santayra and Charleville, *Code rabbinique, Eben Haezer*, 2 vol.: Alger, 1868-69 — J. Simon, *l'Education et l'instruction des enfants chez les anciens Juifs;* Nîmes, 1879. — *Tesoubot hakme Çarfat we Lotair*, réponses faites par de célèbres rabbins français et lorrains des XIe et XIIe siècles, published by Joel Müller; Vienne, 1881.—Isidore Weill, *Philosophie religieuse de Lévi ben Gerson;* Paris, 1868. — Michel A. Weill, *Le Judïsmo, ses dogmes et sa mission;* Paris, 1866-69. — Michel A. Weill, *La Morale du Judaïsme;* Paris, 1875. — Michel A. Weill, *La Parole de Dieu;* Paris, 1880. — Dr M. S. Zuckermandel, *Tosefta nach den Erfurter und Wiener Handschriften;* Pasewalk, 1877-80.

Publications of the Alliance.

The *Alliance* has besides published directly a certain number of works devoted principally to the statistical position of the Jews and the defence of the moral interest of Judaism. Here is the list :

L'Affaire Fornaraki à Alexandrie, Consultation medico légale par P. Brouardel; Paris, 1881. — *L'Affaire Fornaraki à Alexandrie, rapport de la commission d'enquête;* Paris, 1881. — Bluntschli, *L'Etat roumain et la situation légale des Juifs en Roumanie,* traduit de l'allemand et publié par *l'Alliance israélite univ r: elle;* Paris, 1879. — Marco Antonio Canini, *La vérité sur la question israélite en Roumanie;* Paris, 1879. — *Les Conventions commerciales de la Roumanie devant le dioit public curopéen;* Paris, 1878. — *Ueber die bürgerliche Gleichstellung der Israeliten im Aargau;* Aarau, 1862. — J. Halévy, *Prières des Falashas ou Juifs d'Abyssinie;* Paris, 1877. — M. Legoyt, *De certaines immunités biostatiques de la race juive;* Paris, 1868. — Isidore Loeb, *La situation des israélites en Serbie et en Roumanie;* Paris, 1876. — Isidore Lœb, *La situation des israélites en Turquie, en Serbie et en Roumanie;* Paris, 1877. — Mardochée Aby Scrour, *Les Daggatoûn, tribu d'origine juive demeurant dans le désert du Sahara,* traduit de l'hébreu et annoté par Isidore Loeb ; Paris, 1881. — *La Persécution des Israélites en Russie, compte-rendu du meeting public tenu au Mansion House de Londres le mercredi* 1er *février* 1882 ; translated from the English edition published by the Anglo-Jewish Association; Paris, 1882. — *Les Persécutions contre les Israélites roumains en octobre-décembre* 1876 ; Paris, 1877. — *La question juive dans les Chambres roumaines, compte-rendu des séances de la Chambre des Députés et du Sénat du mois de mars 1879;* Paris, 1879. — *Réunion convoquée par l'Alliance israélite universelle en août 1878;* Paris, 1878. — *Réunion en faveur des Israélites de l'Orient tenue à Paris en décembre 1876;* Paris 1876. — M. J. Schleiden, *Les Juifs et la science au moyen âge* truduit de l'allemand et imprimé par *l'Alliance israélite;* Paris, 1877. — *Situation des Israélites in Serbie;* Paris, s. d. (1864?). — Zickel-Kœchlin, *Le traité de commerce entre la France et la Suisse et la liberté des cultes;* Paris, s. d. (1863?).

The *Alliance* publishes, since its foundation, semesterly " Bulletins " in French, and long time ago too in German. It has, for a while, issued semesterly Reports in English and in Hebrew, and sometimes even in Judaïco-Spanish. Since 1873 it publishes a monthly Report in French and German. It thinks of resuming the publication of Reports in English and Hebrew.

Missions.

This question was raised in a previous chapter about the scientific missions of the *Alliance* in Morocco and Abyssinia, in the country of the Falashas. The *Alliance* also contributed towards the expenses of the voyage of Mordoché Aby Serour on the confines of the Sahara.

The Library.

In fine, in 1868, a donation of 10,000 fr. from Mr. L.-M. Rothschild, of London, enabled the *Alliance* to found a Library, which was kept up by an annual subvention, bringing together all the documents and publications concerning the history of the Jews, as well as the different sciences relating to statistics, anthropology, demography, legislation, etc. This Library comprises at the present day nearly 20,000 volumes. It is not only an indispensable instrument for the Society's work, but it is placed at the disposition of all the learned men who occupy themselves with Judaism, who wish to study its history. It is, in fact, one of the creations of which the *Alliance* is the most proud, and which has obtained the greatest success. A legacy of 50,000 fr. from Mr. L.-M. Rothschild will assure its future, and will gain for this noble-minded man our eternal gratitude.

V.

CONCLUSION

It is hardly useful to recall, in this present Report, the steps taken by the *Alliance*, at the epoch of its foundation, before the Ionian Senate, and its favourable reception by that body, for the purpose of safeguarding the rights of the Greek Israelites; the Algerian Israelites, emancipated by the decree of M. Crémieux on the 24th of October, 1870, and to whom the Society came to its aid for the purpose of securing to them their acquired rights; the French Israelites in Switzerland, to whom the treaty of commerce with France, in 1867, procured, at least an efficacious protection which turned to the profit of the Swiss Israelites themselves. When the *Alliance* was founded, the cause of civilization seemed to be assured in most of the European countries, and there appeared every probability that the new Society would not be called upon to occupy itself about it.

The Antisemitism.

The events which followed destroyed these hopes. The civilised world assist, since several years, at a spectacle the least unexpected and the most painful. It was in the face of all Europe the spectacle was witnessed of a sudden revival of the fanaticism of the Middle Ages; all the passions which were supposed to be extinct, all the calumnies which were supposed to have received their condemnation. A detestable literature preached every day hatred of the Jews, war against the Jews, the anti-Semitism has its societies, its comic journals, its illustrated almanacks. The *Alliance israélite* is one of its nightmares, and the number of its falsehoods and deceptions brought against them were simply incalculable. Not one of those who invented these accusations had ever given themselves the trouble to read the reports of the Society, even the bulletins which the *Alliance* distributed every year to the number of 60,000 copies. From this fact only may be measured the veracity and the value of their accusations.

The *Alliance* did not mix itself up in this war. The Israelites, in the countries where they were most attacked, did not want the support of the Society; they contented themselves with combatting single-handed for their honour and their rights, they were right in so doing.

The Tisza Eszlar Case.

One of the most melancholy episodes of this anti-Semitic war was the law-suit of Tisza Eszlar, where several poor Israelites of a village in Hungary were the victims of an odious and ridiculous accusation directed, in fact, against whole Judaism. That the success of such an accusation was possible, no one ever thought of; what astonished every one was that such an accusation should have had birth. The Hungarian tribunals made justice of it. Their verdict could be awaited with security, but it did not in any way discourage those who, in Hungary and elsewhere, continued to breathe forth their hatred and fanaticism. Their impassioned predictions excited minds and awakened every passion.

It is against this fratricidal propaganda that we must struggle without ceasing ; it is against the calumnies always springing up that we must combat.

If the enemies of the Jews are stubborn, we must show them the same stubborness. It is a task which the *Alliance* has imposed on itself since its foundation, and it has only to persevere.

G

There must be no illusion. A breath of intolerance and fanaticism is passing over a great part of Europe, hatreds and prejudices are again stirred up ; the contagion of the evil is extending, from the countries where it raised, over the neighbouring countries, the world is infected by literary productions the most unwholesome, the Jews of every country are being attacked in their honour, it is necessary to act on the defensive.

The centre of the evil, nevertheless, is not in Germany, where the struggle has subsided, but among the nations less civilised, but in younger nations, still in formation. It is the Israelites of Roumania, of Hungary, of Galicia, and of Russia which serve as the sole aim of the enemies of the Jews. It is to those poor populations, the one victims of oppression, the others unfortunate and calumniated, to whom we must stretch out the hand. Their profound misery is a wound always open, and which devours Judaism. This can only be healed by giving them an elementary instruction, an instruction professional and agricultural, in giving them schools, schoolmasters, employers, and rabbis. The task is an immense one, it imposes itself on our good will, it is a work to which we should consecrate all our forces and all our energy.

The work of the Future.

We have seen, by what precedes, what has been the work of the *Alliance* from its foundation to the present day.

This work should be now extended and applied to all the Oriental countries in Europe. In order that the action of the *Alliance* should be what it ought to be, it is necessary : --

To develope the institutions already existing, schools in European and Asiatic Turkey, in Bulgaria, in Roumelia, in

Morocco, and in Tunis; augment the number of professors, apprentices, workshops for young girls, ameliorate
the material, the school-houses, and the programmes of
teaching;

Create analogous institutions in Roumania, in Galicia,
and in Russia;

Encourage more than ever the publications destined to
enlighten public opinion on Judaism and the Jews, and
the refutation of the calumnies of which every day they
are the object. They accumulate, as a means of attack,
mountains of falsehoods and errors : truth will in the end
triumph.

This task is a great one, it demands considerable sacrifices and manly resolution. In order that the *Alliance*
may be able to do this, its resources must be doubled and
even trebled.

It will be the work of the Future!

About one million of Jews are called upon to ensure the
safety of five millions of their co-religionists.

They will not fail in this duty!

CENTRAL COMMITTEE

MEMBERS RESIDING IN PARIS

Messrs.

L. Isidor, Grand-Rabbi of France, *Honorary President.*
S.-H. Goldschmidt, *President.*
Joseph Derenbourg, *Vice-Pres.*
Narcisse Leven, *Vice-President*
E.-S. Kann, *Secretary - General.*
Léonce Lehmann, *Treas.-Deleg.*
E.-A. Astruc, Grand-Rabbi.
G. Bédarrides.
Jules Carvallo.
Abraham Créhange.
Hartwig Derenbourg.
Michel Erlanger.

Messrs.

Baron M. de Hirsch.
Zadoc Kahn, Grand-Rabbi.
Edouard Kohn.
Ernest Lévi-Alvarès.
Théodore Lévy.
Eugène Manuel.
Jules Oppert.
Eugène Pereire.
Joseph Reinach.
Jules Rosenfeld.
Victor Saint-Paul.
Louis Singer.
E.-F.-Vénéziani.

Hippolyte Rodrigues, Honorary Member.

MEMBERS NOT RESIDING IN PARIS

Messrs.

Dr. Adler, Grand-Rabbi, at Cashel.
Dr. Baerwald, at Frankfort-on-the-Main.
Dr. Bamberger, Rabbi, at Kœnigsberg.
Comte A. de Camondo, at Constantinople.
Israel Costa, Rabbi, at Leghorn.
Alexandre-A. Daniels, at Amsterdam.
Samuel Dreyfus-Neumann, at Basle.
Moses-A. Dropsie, at Philadelphia.
Dr. Dunner, Grand-Rabbi of Northern Holland, at Amsterdam.
Dr. Feilchenfeld, Rabbi, at Posen.
Dr. Frank, Rabbi, at Cologne.
Dr. Fuld, lawyer, at Frankfort-on-the-Main.
Dr. Graetz, professor, at Breslau.
Sir Julian Goldsmid. Bart., at London.
Myer-S. Isaacs. at New York.
Dr. Josephthal, solicitor, at Nuremberg.
Eude Lolli, Grand-Rabbi, at Padua.
H. Magnus, at Leipzig.
Maroni, Grand-Rabbi, at Florence.
A. Merzbacher, at Munich.
Dr. S. Neumann, at Berlin.
Dr. Philippson, Rabbi, at Bonn.
Esdra Pontremoli, Rabbi, at Verceil.
Dr. Leone Ravenna, at Ferrara.
Simon C.-Salomon, at Metz.
Dr. A. Salvendi, Rabbi, at Durkheim a. d. H.
Philipp Simon, at Hamburg.
Ritter Joseph de Wertheimer, at Vienna.
Dr. A.-A. Wolff, K. D., Grand-Rabbi, at Copenhagen.

EXTRACT FROM THE STATUTES

OF THE

ALLIANCE ISRAÉLITE UNIVERSELLE

FOUNDED IN 1860

ART. 1. The *Alliance Israélite Universelle* has for object :

1° To labour everywhere for the emancipation and moral progress of the Israelites ;

2° To lend an efficacious support to all those who suffer by their quality of Israelite ;

3° To encourage every kind of publication tending to bring about this result.

ART. 2. To become a member of the Society, the person must give in his adhesion to the Statutes.

ART. 4. The *minimum* of the subscription destined to meet the charges of the Society is fixed at **Six Francs** per annum.

ART. 5. The Society is directed by a Central Committee sitting in Paris.

ART. 6. The number of members composing the Central Committee is fixed at **sixty**.

ART. 8. The Central Committee are named by a universal vote of the members forming the Society by a majority of votes.

ART. 9. The members of the Central Committee are nominated for nine years, renewable by thirds every three years.

ART. 15. A Committee can be constituted in any locality where the Society counts ten adherents.

ART. 16. Regional Committees can be constituted in any country where several local Committees exist.

ART. 17. The regional and local Committees are renewable every year. Outgoing members are indefinitely re-eligible.

ART. 19. They will transmit to the Central Committee and they will receive all communications on every object interesting to the Society.

ART. 20. They will use all their efforts to promote subscriptions, and deposit the same at the cash office of the Central Committee.

TABLE OF CONTENTS

(The Figures indicate the page)

I. OBJECT AND ORGANISATION OF THE SOCIETY.

Object of the work, 2. Excluded questions, 4. Titles and Devise, 5. Means of action, 7. Organisation, 8. Progressive Development, 9. Analogous Societies, 10. The Members, the Budget, 11. The Foundation of M. de Hirsch, 13. Annual Budget, 13. Divers Chapters of the Budget, 15. The coadjutors, 15.

II. THE ISRAELITES IN THE EUROPEAN STATES.

ROUMANIA : General situation, 17. Formation of Roumania, 17. Illusions in regard to Roumania, 17. New legislation, 18. Mr. Crémieux at Bucharest in 1866, 19. Pillage of the Synagogue of Bucharest, 19. New policy, Revolution of 1866, 20. Legal Persecution, 21. The laws of exception, 21. Persecution by riots, 23. Action of the *Alliance*, 23. The European Powers, 24. Artifices of the persecution, 25. Public opinion and the Chambers, 26. Meeting at Paris in 1876, 26. The Berlin Congress, 27. Results of the Congress, 28. Suppression of Article 7 of the Constitution, 28. The actual Situation, 29.

SERVIA : The Situation, 29. The Cause of the Persecutions, 30. Historical, Legislation, 30. Laws of 1856 and 1861, 31. Persecutions, 31. Action of the *Alliance*, 32. The Treaty of Berlin and its effects, 33.

EASTERN ROUMELIA AND BULGARIA, 33.

RUSSIA : Old relations with the *Alliance*, 35. Famine of 1869, 36. Meeting at Berlin, 36. The Kœnigsberg Committee, 37. Work of the Russian apprentices, 37. The great Persecution of 1881—1882, 38. Subscriptions and special Committees, 39. What was to be done ?, 39. Emigration to Palestine impossible, 39. Emigration to America, 40. Charles Netter at Brody, 40. New difficulties, 41. M. Veneziani at Brody, 41. Agricultural colonies in America, 42. Agricultural colonies in Palestine, 42. What of the future?, 43.

III. MUSSULMAN COUNTRIES.

TURKEY: The Government, 44. The Law, 45. Situation of the Israelites, 45. Protection accorded, punishment of outrage, 46. Blood prejudice, 46. Famine, war and fire, 47. The war of 1877, 47. Palestine, 48. Egypt, 49. Tunis and Tripoli, 50.

MOROCCO, 51. Murders and outrages, 52. Protectionist measures and firmans, 53. The Protections, 54. The Conference at Madrid, 54. Aid, 55.

PERSIA: The Situation, 56. H. M. the Shah in Europe, 57.

IV. SCHOOLS, APPRENTICESHIP, SCIENTIFIC WORK.

PRIMARY SCHOOLS AND APPRENTICESHIP: Aim of the Schools, 59. Extension of the Schools, 57. Utility of the Schools. 59. Moral results, 60, Material results, 61. History of the Schools, 61. Girls' Schools, 62. Apprenticeship of the boys, 63. Importance of the Schools, 64. School houses, 66. Scholastic material, 66. The Talmud-Toras, 66. The School at Jerusalem, 67. Preparatory Schools, 68.

THE AGRICULTURAL SCHOOL OF JAFFA: History of its foundation, 69. Charles Netter at Jaffa, 70. First state of the School, 71. Progress of the School, 73. Actual state of the School, 74.

SCIENTIFIC WORK: Prizes, 76. Subvention, 86. Publications of the Alliance, 78. Missions, 79. The Library, 79.

V. CONCLUSION.

The Antisemitism, 80. The Tisza-Eszlar case, 80. The work of the future, 82.

The members of the Central Committee, 85.

Extract from the Statutes of the Alliance israélite universelle, 86.

Printed on January, 1885.

The Secretary : ISIDORE LOEB.

Paris.—Printed by Ch. Maréchal et J. Montorier, 16, passage des Petites Ecuries

www.ingramcontent.com/pod-product-compliance
Lightning Source LLC
Chambersburg PA
CBHW020306090426

42735CB00009B/1234

* 9 7 8 3 3 3 7 0 6 1 6 3 0 *